EMPOWERED CHURCH LEADERSHIP

Ministry in the Spirit
According to Paul

BRIAN J. DODD

InterVarsity Press
Downers Grove, Illinois

InterVarsity Press
P.O. Box 1400, Downers Grove, IL 60515-1426
World Wide Web: www.ivpress.com
E-mail: mail@ivpress.com

InterVarsity Press® is the book-publishing division of InterVarsity Christian Fellowship/USA®, a student
movement active on campus at hundreds of universities, colleges and schools of nursing in the United States
of America, and a member movement of the International Fellowship of Evangelical Students. For information
about local and regional activities, write Public Relations Dept., InterVarsity Christian Fellowship/USA,
6400 Schroeder Rd., P.O. Box 7895, Madison, WI 53707-7895, or visit the IVCF website at <www.ivcf.org>.

Cover design: Cindy Kiple

Cover and interior image: Nick Gunderson/Getty Images

ISBN 0-8308-2392-1

Printed in the United States of America ∞

Library of Congress Cataloging-in-Publication Data

Dodd, Brian J., 1960-
    Empowered church leadership: ministry in the spirit according to
    Paul / Brian J. Dodd.
        p. cm.
Includes bibliographical references and index.
    ISBN 0-8308-2392-1
    1. Christian leadership. 2. Bible. N.T. Epistles of
Paul—Criticism, interpretation, etc. 3. Paul, the Apostle, Saint. I. Title.
BV652.1.D63 2003
253—dc21
                                                            2003008230

| P | 19 | 18 | 17 | 16 | 15 | 14 | 13 | 12 | 11 | 10 | 9 | 8 | 7 | 6 | 5 | 4 | 3 | 2 | 1 |
| Y | 18 | 17 | 16 | 15 | 14 | 13 | 12 | 11 | 10 | 09 | 08 | 07 | 06 | 05 | 04 | 03 |

To the memory of my father, Asa,

and to my mother, Mildred,

my brother, Jim,

and my sister, Suzanne

CONTENTS

1 Spirit-Empowered Leadership. 9

2 Followership and Self-Surrender. 31

3 Pay the Price, Carry the Cross. 61

4 God's Power in Cracked Pots 79

5 The Power of Personal Example 93

6 The Power of Partners 104

7 Through Prayer 121

8 The Race to the Bottom 139

9 The Leadership We Need Is Apostolic 149

Appendix: Hearing God's Direction for Your Ministry 159

Notes. 181

Indexes 187

1

SPIRIT-EMPOWERED
LEADERSHIP

> *Alas for those who go down to Egypt for help*
> *and who rely on horses,*
> *who trust in chariots because they are many*
> *and in horsemen because they are very strong,*
> *but do not look to the Holy One of Israel*
> *or consult the LORD!*

> ISAIAH 31:1

EVERY SQUARE METER OF THE PLANET has its own satellite address, called its geocode. These precise addresses materialized because of the American military drive to be able to land laser-guided bombs down chimneys. Now an average citizen, if he or she is willing to spend enough money, can have a personal version of the global positioning system (GPS) in a car's dashboard. The GPS computer will tell a driver how far to the next turn, display the map of where the person is and plot the quickest route to the desired destination. One version even talks to the driver in a computerized voice: "Turn around immediately. You are going the wrong way."

The GPS works from the ancient sailing principle of triangulation. On the open sea, without reference points or a compass, a ship hopelessly drifts in unknown directions. When one is traveling great distances, even a degree off course can result in landing hundreds of miles from one's destination. An ancient mariner determined location and course by creating a triangle between the ship and two other fixed points (hence the term *triangulation*). During the day visible land was essential. On clear nights, the stars provided all sorts of fixed points by which position could be determined. In the technological age, a traveler needs only to be able to read a computer-generated map that decodes position by triangulating from the GPS satellite system.

Anyone who wants to find God's path and direction knows the need for a reference point. Without God's positioning, we are adrift on the open sea. With no fixed reference points around us, with only floating values, opinions and competing goals, we cannot navigate a sure course. We need eternal reference points, God's Word and God's will. This need has never been greater for leaders of the Christian church in the West. We often have neglected God's great Global Positioning System, and we have found ourselves drifting along with the wind.

This lack of a divine reference point is all too obvious in the burgeoning market of leadership books and seminars. We have hungered after the world's wisdom and stuffed ourselves on secular practices, techniques and buzzwords. A caricature of this trend appeared in a recent news article, which reported that leaders of two declining mainline denominations had gathered at the Disney Institute: "Speakers from the Disney Institute have been urging the local church leaders to think more creatively to stem declining memberships."[1] What? Mickey Mouse is going to help us shore up our slumping market share? All this in the face of the fact that churches devoted to scriptural Christianity are the only ones experiencing growth. This made the old joke hit too close to home for me: "What's the difference between the church and Disneyland? Disneyland has the *real* Mickey Mouse!"

This trend to rely on secular leadership strategies, to equate ministry with management, has affected and infected the thinking of almost an entire generation of Christian leaders. In the early 1980s, when I first began picking up books on leadership, my motivation was simple. I wanted to be more effective as a local church pastor. The people in my church were not where they needed to be — in my view — and I was not sure how to get them from where they were to where I thought they should be. So I turned to the leadership gurus, unaware that much of what they were teaching from secular leadership principles was quite contrary to the kingdom leadership principles Jesus taught and Paul embodied.

The lure of success is seductive. Its siren song causes so many people to uncritically ascribe so much authority to high-profile leaders, platform speakers and megachurch pastors. They appear to be successful (read: are in charge of a lot of people and money), so what they say must be authoritative. In the United States, this high value placed on success is alien to the value the kingdom of God places on faithfulness and obedience. In American measurement, Jesus' human life was a failure because it ended in the shame and disgrace on a cross with all his followers abandoning him.

I bought into the trend for a time, and something strange happened to me in the process. I had become a bit like the frog in the proverbial kettle. I was learning about the latest innovations in leadership, but I was unaware of the rising heat that could cook my spirit. In my simpler days, I had learned that the crucified and risen One was the focus of the church and that "the message about the cross is foolishness to those who are perishing, but to us who are being saved it is the power of God" (1 Cor 1:18).

I did not find this message in the books I was reading (and I read just about everything—really). But slowly, subtly and for a time, a focus on vision, excellence and seeker sensitivity had replaced the cross in my thinking. My ministry reflected my thinking, up to date but powerless. I am not claiming it is anyone's fault but my own. By my own doing, I was drifting, awash in leadership lingo and principles but often ignoring and even navigating against the way of Jesus, the way of the cross and the way of the kingdom of God.

I realize now that I am not the only one this happened to. All around us we can find examples of a sellout to the ways of the world. One example will suffice. I have in front of me as I am writing this a several-page letter from a church executive. The letterhead has "Committed to Excellence" prominently displayed, but there is no mention of Jesus in this letter on ministry development. If I were a Martian and landed in the middle of the Oakland Raiders' stadium, I would think the letter and the stadium were part of the same organization. "Commitment to Excellence" is the Raiders' motto, and it is displayed throughout the Oakland Coliseum. In my experience with this church executive's corporate culture, the real values are much like those of the Raiders' owner, Al Davis: "Just win, baby!" Their organization's expansion is far more important than the expansion of the kingdom. Is it difficult to see what is so obvious? We have met the enemy, and the enemy is us!

As I look back, the reason I came to Jesus in the first place was not because of some polished leader or excellence of the church but because I had a spiritual awakening. God acted in a sovereign way, and I met the risen Savior whom the church preached: "For Jews demand signs and Greeks desire wisdom, but we proclaim Christ crucified, a stumbling block to Jews and foolishness to Gentiles, but to those who are the called, both Jews and Greeks, Christ the power of God and the wisdom of God" (1 Cor 1:22-24).

I hadn't been impressed into a relationship with God. I had been called into it. The call came from outside me. All at once, in the middle of my conscious life, there stood the living Lord Jesus, touching me, healing me, transforming me, beckoning me to follow in his steps.

But much later, as a pastor, I fell into no shortage of leadership seminars, books and tapes—Christian and otherwise. They dazzled and excited me, a weary warrior of the faith, promising new energy, renewed effectiveness and fulfillment of dreams. But many, if not most, Christian leadership books today are hardly Christian apart from proof-texting use of Scripture and application to church life. Distinctively Christian hallmarks of leadership found in the Bible are all but absent most of the time in popular Christian literature: the cross, self-sacrificial servanthood, love and gentleness, Spirit-led and Spirit-empowered ministry through weak vessels, prayer, suffering, and the like. Instead, the growth industry of leadership literature tends to be peppered with stories about McDonald's and Wal-Mart. Whatever happened to Jesus, Peter and Paul?[2] I needed to hear Isaiah's ancient warning: "Alas for those who go down to Egypt for help / and who rely on horses, / who trust in chariots because they are many / and in horsemen because they are very strong, / but do not look to the Holy One of Israel / or consult the LORD!" (Is 31:1).

I was negotiating with Egypt, not consulting the Lord. I was not discerning enough to put the leadership literature I was reading into a spiritual context. What I needed was a spiritual director, not more secular leadership books dressed up as Christian teaching. I needed encouragement and accountability to pray, not strategies for motivating people in the direction I wanted them to go. After all, what good is getting people to follow you if you have not received marching orders from your Lord? Too often I was experiencing the power of Dodd, not the power of God. Paul diagnoses this dilemma as the difference between living "according to the flesh" rather than "according to the Spirit." I'll have more to say on this in chapter two.

After several years of imbibing all the leadership books and seminars I could find, I returned to school to study for a Ph.D. in New Testament on Paul's style of leadership. To my embarrassment, I began with the approach "from the flesh," seeking human and social explanations for Paul's effectiveness as a leader. There was no doubt Paul was effective as a Christian leader. I wondered what timeless tricks he had learned from leaders around him that we can use too. My initial research question was, "What social and cultural influences on Paul's style of leadership can we demonstrate?" What had Paul learned and adapted from the Pharisees, the civic leadership of the empire, Roman military leadership, the Cynic philosophers, Greco-Roman rhetoricians, the prophets, Moses and Abraham? I soon got my fill and discovered my outline would not work as a dissertation project (thank God!). In the end, I submitted a thesis that focused on a crucial yet partial aspect of Paul's leadership style: his use of modeling and personal example for those who are "in Christ."[3]

What was striking about Paul's leadership was not the ways that it reflected the effective leadership style of the people in his day. In fact, what was so impressive was the uniquely Christ-centered and cross-reflecting style of leadership that he exhibited. Theologians might call these christocentric and cruciform aspects of his leadership. This study of Paul yielded diamonds I had not anticipated. Instead of focusing on Paul's culture and human elements of leadership, what continually leaped off the page was how a Christian leader is to reflect the gospel he or she preaches. We are to preach the cross, *and* our lives are to conform to the image of Jesus in his death and resurrection. I rediscovered that people need not polished leaders but faithful witnesses who point them to the crucified and risen One—by their words and by their lives. What leaders need most are not new techniques but an awareness of the Spirit's direction, the importance of prayer and the essentially team nature of effective ministry (in New Testament terms, the "body life" nature of effective ministry). During this time of extended Bible study, the things that fed my spirit were the uniquely biblical and Christ-centered aspects of the leadership of Paul. I had come full circle.

When I began sharing leadership insights from Paul's letters with other Christian leaders, I realized they too were starving for an essentially Christian theology of leadership. In fact, the motivation for this book was born out of a retreat I was leading with about fifty pastors. Their unanswered longings were front and center in Paul's explanation of godly, effective leadership. They asked questions such as, Why is it so hard to serve Jesus sometimes? Why is it so painful to be a leader? Why do people take unfair shots at Christian leaders? Why is there so little power and dynamic fruit of the Spirit in my ministry? These aren't questions the Christian clones of secular leadership consultants are answering, but Paul had anticipated them. Indeed, he had lived through what I have come to see as the shared experience of most faithful, godly leaders. Much of what I have written here, I have road-tested with practitioners of Christian leadership. A lot of it comes out of my painful learning experiences. I believe I have stuck to the crucial matters.

What follows is a careful and close reading of Paul's letters by someone who is deeply interested in leadership development, passionately committed to church renewal and extension, somewhat experienced in pastoral ministry, widely read in leadership literature and academically trained in New Testament studies. I have wanted this to be an aid to leaders, lay and clergy alike, rooted clearly and solidly in biblical, theological soil. I have worked at focusing on takeaway value, so that each chapter with its discussion questions can be used with leadership boards, leadership retreats, in classes and in Bible studies. My prayer for this book is that it will help emerging and developing leaders to closely read the compass of Scripture as they chart their future course.

Whenever we read the Bible closely enough to do us any good we should find that the Bible reads us. If we are paying careful attention to a scriptural understanding of leadership we can't ignore the implied criticism that today's church needs something more, something different, something other than what we are usually offered in contemporary leadership studies. There is a pervasive powerlessness and shrinkage of the church in the West. The leadership lessons from the world have not improved our market share, and the sell-out to pragmatism, the heresy of valuing whatever works, has not worked. The kingdom we are building is essentially different from Wal-Mart and the Mormon Church. To the extent that our leadership practices reflect the ways of the world, if we evaluate them fairly, they haven't worked. Each week fifty-three thousand Christians leave the church in the West,[4] and the United States is now the fifth most unchurched nation on the planet.[5] Many of those churches that gain attenders may be getting people through the door, but it is apparent that the gospel does not penetrate their lives or the culture. A new generation of Spirit-empowered leaders is needed— right here, right now.

The best place to look for a renewed understanding of leadership is in the pages of Scripture. One wonders if much of Christian leadership literature is a Trojan horse from the enemy camp, since so little space is spent on what the Bible says. Paul's words to Timothy are still true: "All scripture is inspired by God and is useful for teaching, for reproof, for correction, and for training in righteousness, so that everyone who belongs to God may be proficient, equipped for every good work" (2 Tim 3:16-17).

If we are to be equipped for "every good work" of ministry and leadership, we need to have mastered Paul's extended biblical and theological underpinnings for leadership. We need to dig deeper into the Bible, not rummage elsewhere for what leaders need. This book is meant to

engage the reader in an extended study of the New Testament's underpinnings for effective, life-giving leadership.

Is Paul's Example a Better Option?

Holding up Paul's example for emulation has its problems for some
readers and needs a brief justification. When we encounter the teaching of this ancient apostle, some issues disqualify him from the contemporary court of admiration. Among these concerns are his attitudes and
teaching about women, his silence on the abolition of slavery and his
apparently rigid and dogmatic insistence on traditional morality. I have
dealt with these and other objections at length in *The Problem with Paul*
and refer the reader there for a more extended treatment of these persistent questions.[6] My approach is to evaluate Paul from his cultural point
of view and to acknowledge that he was extremely progressive, even lib-
eral, with regard to women in leadership and the place of slaves in the
church (consider Phoebe, Priscilla and Junia in Romans 16, to name a
few). Indeed, it was among women and slaves that the early church
spread the fastest. Though Paul comes off to people in our day as polit-
ically incorrect in many ways, a fair reading of him in light of his ancient
cultural heritage gives a wholly more favorable impression.

Instead of measuring Paul's views against our modern sensibilities,
a few relevant questions for the topic of this book are, Would you hire
Paul to lead your church or ministry? Would his qualities and values
put him on your short list for hiring? Before we answer too quickly, we
should realize that many people in Paul's day had difficulties with his
manner and style of leadership. In fact, we can list many qualities that
people then thought disqualified him from his central leadership role
as an apostle.

1. *Paul was a poor public speaker by the social standards of his day.* "I
   did not come with eloquence or superior wisdom as I proclaimed to

you the testimony of God" (1 Cor 2:1 NIV). His critics bluntly dismissed him with, "For they say, 'His letters are weighty and strong, but his bodily presence is weak, and his speech contemptible'" (2 Cor 10:10). Mind you, this is how *Paul* reports their criticism of him!

2. *He had obvious physical deformities that cast a shadow over his leadership abilities.* Greco-Roman culture, much like image-obsessed America, emphasized physical form and stature as a measure of a person's standing in society and leadership. Paul did not measure up, and he notes with delight how the Galatians overcame their cultural baggage by receiving him: "You know that it was because of a physical infirmity that I first announced the gospel to you; though my condition put you to the test, you did not scorn or despise me, but welcomed me as an angel of God, as Christ Jesus" (Gal 4:13-14).

3. *He disavowed his human qualities and abilities as insignificant compared with the power that comes from knowing Jesus.* Paul was capable, educated, of the right pedigree and with incredible passion and dedication (see Phil 3:3-5). Yet he had learned as he walked with Christ in his new relationship. "Whatever gains I had, these I have come to regard as loss because of Christ" (Phil 3:7). Paul had come to see that all these human abilities and qualities, while regarded highly by those not walking in the Spirit, were a deficit and a liability. The true source of life-giving leadership flowed from who Christ is and what he does through his leaders and people.

4. *He had a pattern of supporting himself with secular work* and receiving support from some churches (Philippi) but not others (Corinth). An integral part of his society was the practice of patronage, in which a patron financially supported his or her client and received admiration by affiliation when that client excelled. In some ways, it is much like how a supporter of a professional sports team derives a sense of

accomplishment when that team wins even though the supporter has done nothing from the armchair to win the game. Paul's pattern of self-support through tent making denied the Corinthians a sense of ownership in his ministry.

5. *He was confrontational, controversial and not ashamed of it (Gal 2; Acts 15).* Paul's attitude in Galatians 1–2 is "I know when I am right. Even if Peter or an angel from heaven insists on circumcision to be saved, I will face them down." The velvet glove of gentleness Paul wore thinly veiled his steel hand when a crucial issue was at stake (2 Cor 10:1; 1 Thess 2:7).

6. *He had a jail record.* Multiple offenses. And rioting seemed to follow him everywhere he went. That was *after* he had become a Christian! Before that, he confessed he had participated in the murdering of Christians: "even though I was formerly a blasphemer, a persecutor, and a man of violence" (1 Tim 1:13). He even changed his name from Saul to Paul, perhaps in part to lessen the violent associations that "Saul" conjured among Christians (see, for example, Acts 9:13-14). Is this the man you would want as the chief administrative officer of your church? Paul had to appeal more than once to his friends not to be ashamed of his imprisonment (2 Tim 1:8). No one could call Paul a hypocrite—because he first admitted he was the worst sinner of all (1 Tim 1:15; Greek *prōtos*, meaning "first" or "foremost" sinner).

This is not exactly the resume of the upstanding citizen-leader. Why was Paul so effective when he had so much going against him? To what could he attribute his success and effectiveness throughout the Roman Empire?

Fortunately, Paul addressed this issue directly, and we do not have to speculate on his self-understanding on this matter. For Paul, the secret to his success was beyond human skills, techniques or principles. How did he account for his success as one who did not measure up to society's expectations of leaders and public figures? His explanation goes further than what we might think. He doesn't simply say, "Wow, look what God did through me. Isn't God amazing?" This is part of his message, but it has more of an edge to it than this. Paul says the reason God used such an unlikely leader as him is the same reason God was drawing the lowly people of the planet into the kingdom. God's purpose is to overthrow the worldly focus that we humans put on appearance and accomplishment and abilities apart from God. Instead,

> God chose what is foolish in the world to shame the wise; God chose what is weak in the world to shame the strong; God chose what is low and despised in the world, things that are not, to reduce to nothing things that are, so that no one might boast in the presence of God. He is the source of your life in Christ Jesus, who became for us wisdom from God, and righteousness and sanctification and redemption, in order that, as it is written, "Let the one who boasts, boast in the Lord." (1 Cor 1:27-31)

The whole point is this. God uses Paul, and the Corinthians—and ordinary people like you and me—to overturn the approach of human pride, the part of us that wants to pull ourselves up by our bootstraps and take the credit for ourselves. At the sinful core of each of us is a spiritual two-year-old who wants to "do it by myself." This is our problem. The solution is for us to learn to rely upon God, to live in radical dependence upon God's saving help and daily assistance. If we have something to boast about, it is to boast in the Captain of our faith, Jesus Christ. Pride, arrogance and haughtiness are enemies of empowered ministry. God is pleased to dwell in the humble.

If able human leadership could solve the serious problems that human sinfulness has created in our world, it would have done so by now.

The problem is greater than a need for new vision or new direction. We are not simply going the wrong way as a people; we are "dead in our sins," powerless to change our predicament (Rom 5:6). We need more than good leadership. We need a Savior so strong that he can absorb the shockwave of sin in himself and resurrect us from the death-trap existence we are living. Without Jesus—whether we have good leaders or bad leaders—we are without help or hope. The Roman Empire had powerful leaders, but they have all vanished. The early church had dubious leadership (think of each disciple and character in the story!), yet the Christian church continues to expand faster than ever, even when we include the decline of the church in the western hemisphere.

God's way is to freely offer a solution to our plight: salvation from our sin-filled state, forgiveness and hope in the death and resurrection of Jesus. This Paul calls "grace," God's merciful solution to our intractable human condition. Paul says *this* is why God chose to use a star sinner like Paul as a leader for his church:

> *I am grateful to Christ Jesus our Lord, who has strengthened me, because he judged me faithful and appointed me to his service, even though I was formerly a blasphemer, a persecutor, and a man of violence. But I received mercy because I had acted ignorantly in unbelief, and the grace of our Lord overflowed for me with the faith and love that are in Christ Jesus. The saying is sure and worthy of full acceptance, that Christ Jesus came into the world to save sinners—of whom I am the foremost. But for that very reason I received mercy, so that in me, as the foremost [sinner], Jesus Christ might display the utmost patience, making me an example to those who would come to believe in him for eternal life. To the King of the ages, immortal, invisible, the only God, be honor and glory forever and ever. Amen.*
> (1 Tim 1:12-17)

So Paul is a model leader in every way. His dramatic change from violent religious bigot to forgiven messenger for Jesus is itself a picture of the new world order that Jesus brings. Paul as a fallen-forgiven leader embodies what God wants the world to know about Jesus: he pours out mercy, grace and love on failed people. He saves us from our sins, picks us up from the dust of death and sets our feet on a solid place to stand. Our sinful side is deprived of its worst poison, pride. Anyone who stands before God does so by God's merciful action, not by human achievement. Grace, mercy and love are seen in God's choice of Paul as a leader.

Spirit-Empowered Ministry

God's whole agenda is to reconcile a prideful and rebellious humanity to himself. His plan, says Paul, is to choose unlikely leaders so that it will be obvious God is at work. This is the divine incognito, God hiding in the weak things to offend human pride so offensive to the holy God. Anyone who approaches God must do so humbly, gratefully, in recognition that God has mercifully replaced the death that comes from pride with life that comes through God's Spirit.

The leadership secret to Paul's success was not, therefore, located in Paul's specific behaviors, superior character or special techniques. Paul's effectiveness was a God thing. God moved in Paul's ministry. When Paul showed up, God chose to show up in the powerful presence of his Holy Spirit. Paul was completely aware of the secret of his success: "For I will not venture to speak of anything except what Christ has accomplished through me to win obedience from the Gentiles, by word and deed, by the power of signs and wonders, by the power of the Spirit of God, so that from Jerusalem and as far around as Illyricum I have fully proclaimed the good news of Christ" (Rom 15:18-19).

Paul had it clear in his mind why he was effective. He couldn't set up "Paul's School on the Seven Laws of Leadership." There was only one principle that leaders needed to know: God is building a kingdom with his reconciled humanity and universe. Only God could do such a thing. Human efforts, on their own, without God's power, amount to nothing. God invites us to join him in this kingdom-building task.

This is no small theme in Paul's self-descriptions of his leadership and ministry in his letters: "And I came to you in weakness and in fear and in much trembling. My speech and my proclamation were not with plausible words of wisdom, but with a demonstration of the Spirit and of power, so that your faith might rest not on human wisdom but on the power of God" (1 Cor 2:3-5).

Lest we think this applied to Paul alone and not us, remember how he describes all ministry, and therefore all leadership, as dependent upon the Spirit's gifting and empowerment:

> *Now there are varieties of gifts, but the same Spirit; and there are varieties of services, but the same Lord; and there are varieties of activities, but it is the same God who activates all of them in everyone. To each is given the manifestation of the Spirit for the common good. To one is given through the Spirit the utterance of wisdom, and to another the utterance of knowledge according to the same Spirit, to another faith by the same Spirit, to another gifts of healing by the one Spirit, to another the working of miracles, to another prophecy, to another the discernment of spirits, to another various kinds of tongues, to another the interpretation of tongues. All these are activated by one and the same Spirit, who allots to each one individually just as the Spirit chooses. For just as the body is one and has many members, and all the members of the body, though many, are one body, so it is with Christ. For in the one Spirit we were all baptized into one body—Jews or Greeks, slaves or free—and we were all made to drink of one Spirit. (1 Cor 12:4-13)*

The phrases pile up to remind us that ministry and effective work for God do not originate with us but are "by the Spirit," "through the Spirit," "in the Spirit," because of God's Spirit. Any human pride in self-originating accomplishment is dashed on the rocks of this spiritual reality. The world and all who are in it are messed up. The only real help comes from on high. We are truly serving God and God's purposes only when we join what God is doing through his Spirit. We are fortunate vessels to be chosen for the job, taken off the shelf and employed in God's service. We are the pots, God is the potter, and the Spirit is God's presence and power, God himself poured out in and through us.[7]

The Holy Spirit is the key to Paul's success. That partly explains why this is *not* a hot topic among leadership books and seminars in the pragmatic West. You cannot bottle and sell the Holy Spirit. As Jesus says, "The Spirit blows where it chooses, and you hear its voice, but you do not know where it is coming from or where it is heading. So it is with everyone born of the Spirit" (Jn 3:8). The growth of the kingdom and the expansion of the church are works of God by the power of the Holy Spirit. God takes ordinary people and breathes his Spirit into them, and they accomplish amazing things. But God chooses whom, when and where to blow his Spirit.

We all know of abuses of purported gifts and supposed workings of the Holy Spirit. Religious shams have always been around. This is enough to make anyone nervous. But the Reformation principle is still sound: the abuse of a thing doesn't nullify its use. Because there have been lunatics and liars who have abused the gifts and teaching on the Holy Spirit, this doesn't change this one crucial fact: Paul's ministry, and the ministry of the early church for that matter, was a ministry characterized by Spirit-endowed power. The Holy Spirit's power is the key to Paul's success. He says so, over and over again: "Indeed, we live as human beings, but we do not wage war according to human standards; for the weapons of our warfare are not merely human, but they have divine power to destroy strongholds. We destroy arguments and every proud obstacle raised up against the knowledge of God, and we take every thought captive to obey Christ" (2 Cor 10:3-5).

Some interpreters want to focus our attention in this passage on the rhetorical terms for effective argumentation being employed here. But Paul's point is consistent with his self-understanding of why his words and ministry carry such a potent wallop: it is "divine power" that enables him, that causes his argumentation with his opponents to be effective. This is what he says earlier to the Thessalonians: "because our message of the gospel came to you not in word only, but also in power and in the Holy Spirit and with full conviction . . . for in spite of persecution you received the word with joy inspired by the Holy Spirit" (1 Thess 1:5-6). I'm sure this is what he had in mind in 2 Corinthians 10 as well.

A couple of chapters later in 2 Corinthians, he has to address the same issue from a different point of view. His opponents' attack is based on a simple equation: since Paul has all sorts of obvious problems and difficulties, there is no possible way Paul could be speaking for God. Paul's response to this frontal attack is again to remind his Corinthian readers that his difficulties, his weakness and his problems qualify him for the kind of ministry God wants done. God wants to overturn any pretension that God's way is to work through slick leaders, that God works in the same way Hollywood does.

> But he said to me, "My grace is sufficient for you, for power is made perfect in weakness." So, I will boast all the more gladly of my weaknesses, so that the power of Christ may dwell in me. Therefore I am content with weaknesses, insults, hardships, persecutions, and calamities for the sake of Christ; for whenever I am weak, then I am strong. (2 Cor 12:9-10)

Paul doesn't deny their point. He *is* weak, opposed and prone to hardships of every kind. He goes on to agree with his opponents that he is nothing (2 Cor 12:11). But none of this matters to Paul, since the key to his success is not Paul's attributes but the sovereign working of the Holy Spirit: "The signs of a true apostle were performed among you with utmost patience, signs and wonders and mighty works" (2 Cor 12:12).

Paul's power came from above. He was a servant of the living God, who had anointed and empowered Paul in extraordinary ways by the Holy Spirit. The Spirit was a crucial part of his self-understanding of his effectiveness and a key component in his theology. To the Galatians, he writes:

> *The only thing I want to learn from you is this: Did you receive the Spirit by doing the works of the law or by believing what you heard? Are you so foolish? Having started with the Spirit, are you now ending with the flesh? Did you experience so much for nothing?—if it really was for nothing. Well then, does God supply you with the Spirit and work miracles among you by your doing the works of the law, or by your believing what you heard? (Gal 3:2-4)*

I wonder if this searching question in verse 3 should be mounted on every Christian leader's desk: "*Having started with the Spirit, are you now ending with the flesh?*" Each of us began our walk with God by his choice, his action, his initiative. We were "born of the Spirit," to use Jesus' explanation of this turnaround in our relationship with God (Jn 3). If we drift from that empowered place, if we "end with the flesh," we gut the gospel of its transforming and marvelous power. When we fill up the space with our self-will and our determinations to "do it my way," the presence and power of the Spirit are pushed out. Paul says as much: "Live by the Spirit, I say, and do not gratify the desires of the flesh. For what the flesh desires is opposed to the Spirit, and what the Spirit desires is opposed to the flesh; for these are opposed to each other, to prevent you from doing what you want. But if you are led by the Spirit, you are not subject to the law" (Gal 5:16-18).

The Christian life is to be a Spirit-led life, and Christian leadership must be Spirit-led, too. Seminars are stimulating, but the Spirit is where the power comes from. Principles help us stay in control, but the Spirit directs us to what God wants us to do.

But Spirit-led, Spirit-empowered leadership was not just Paul's idea. The pre-Christian Paul faced Christians who displayed a power and spiritual anointing on their ministries. Luke gives a snapshot of how they did things: "With great power the apostles gave their testimony to the resurrection of the Lord Jesus, and great grace was upon them all" (Acts 4:33). That power was first demonstrated in their ability to be understood by hearers in other languages at Pentecost (Acts 2:11). Then Peter healed a cripple by the Holy Spirit's power and he asked the people, "You Israelites, why do you wonder at this, or why do you stare at us, as though by our own power or piety we had made him walk?" (Acts 3:12; see Acts 4:7). Stephen, "full of grace and power, did great wonders and signs among the people" (Acts 6:8). And the amazing story multiplies their example in the book of Acts. All their opponents could think to do to stop them was appeal to carnal power, secular authority, coercive force. When Stephen was stoned to death, Paul stood watching approvingly, tending the coats of the executioners. Nevertheless, the power of the Spirit adorned their work and spurred them on against tremendous opposition and persecution. The whole purpose was to draw attention to the new revelation of God's presence and power among his people. According to Luke, this is the kind of ministry Jesus had promised to his first disciples: "But you will receive power when the Holy Spirit has come upon you; and you will be my witnesses in Jerusalem, in all Judea and Samaria, and to the ends of the earth" (Acts 1:8).

Before he promised an empowered ministry to them, Jesus modeled it for them. He had continually manifested God's divine power, the resurrection being the climax and showcase that God was working in a powerful and unique way in Jesus: "You that are Israelites, listen to what I have to say: Jesus of Nazareth, a man attested to you by God with deeds of power, wonders, and signs that God did through him among you, as you yourselves know. . . . But God raised him up, having freed him from death, because it was impossible for him to be held in its power" (Acts 2:22, 24; cf. Acts 10:38).

It is no wonder then that Paul immediately inherited this same Spirit-empowered approach to leadership. It didn't start with him or the early disciples or even with Jesus. The early disciples realized this had been how God was working through his appointed leaders for a long, long time. The early church traced divine empowerment for leadership all the way back to Moses. "So Moses was instructed in all the wisdom of the Egyptians and was powerful in his words and deeds" (Acts 7:22). God's empowered leaders had been appointed and anointed throughout the ages. So it was with Moses, David, Jeremiah, Jesus, Peter and Paul. So it can be with you and me.

You and I Can Have That Same Empowered Ministry

Cessationists are people who believe that miracles and the sensational spiritual gifts of the Bible were for back then but not for now. All that power ceased with the first apostles, hence the name *cessationist*. This is a theological position found almost exclusively in the materialistic West, and it is virtually incomprehensible in two-thirds of the world where Christians are accustomed to witnessing the movement of the Holy Spirit in power. If cessasionists are right, why did Paul tell Titus, "This Spirit he poured out on us richly through Jesus Christ our Savior" (Tit 3:6)? How can we think the Spirit was for then but not for now? The Spirit gives each Christian all three parts of the trilogy of power, love and self-discipline: "For God did not give us a spirit of cowardice, but rather a spirit of power and of love and of self-discipline" (1 Tim 1:7). Yes, love and self-discipline are crucial components, but we should not conveniently overlook the necessity of the power supplied by God's Spirit. A biblical theology of leadership has to begin here, and an effective ministry must continually "be led by the Spirit." Wherever the church is alive and growing in the world, all these observations are the mother's milk, the ABCs of ministry. Only in the hyper-rationalistic, overly materialistic West, where the church struggles most, are these obvious scriptural truths challenged.

Paul anticipated these days we live in, when immorality would spread like cancer and the church would hold "to the outward form of godliness but deny its power"(2 Tim 3:5). This describes too many of the stale Christian churches of today. Don't the words ring too true? The shoe fits much of my ministry and that of many of the churches that I have experienced. What we need from our leaders and in our churches is not new principles, new ideas or new buildings. What we need is a renewed dependence on God, to be renewed in the person, presence and power of the Holy Spirit. The Holy Spirit, better than any of us, knows how to draw attention to the crucified and risen Jesus, in whom we have life and hope and salvation.

Paul's teaching and example of Spirit-empowered leadership is what this book is about. I break the chapters that follow into three sections. The first section is about where the power comes from. We all have to begin our relationship with God with self-surrender. What is needed is a renewal of followership more than leadership (chap. 2). Chapter three addresses the necessity of suffering, of "carrying the cross," for godly, effective leaders. Chapter four explores the crucial leadership characteristic of being a cracked pot. You could say that these chapters are all about the Potter and the dependency of clay-pot leaders to get their form and usefulness from our Creator God's artful hand.

In the next section, two chapters are devoted to discussing the power we have as leaders because we have come "into Christ": the power of personal example (chap. 5), and the power of partnership, teamwork and multiplying one's ministry by reproducing leaders (chap. 6). When Christ comes into our lives, we come into a new sphere, which Paul calls "in Christ." To be "in Christ" is to be a new creation (2 Cor 5:17), to come into a dual citizenship, one foot on earth, yet complete loyalty to heaven. To be "in Christ" means that our character undergoes transformation, and we become a part of a new people, the body of Christ. Because of this, the example we set and the team we build have divine impact.

In the third section, I devote two chapters to how Paul says we continue to "live by the Spirit." Chapter seven focuses on the crucial need for prayer. Chapter eight reminds us that God works from the bottom up, through the most unlikely people. These two things are essential for leaders today to truly follow and clearly reflect the life of God in Jesus Christ our Lord.

Chapter nine describes the new breed of frontline leaders that I see God raising up in these days, and it describes how we can join with what God is doing in our land. The title of the appendix that follows is self-explanatory: "Hearing God's Direction for Your Ministry."

But first, we must go back to the beginning of the matter.

FOLLOWERSHIP AND SELF-SURRENDER

*Such is the confidence that we have through Christ toward God.
Not that we are competent of ourselves to claim anything
as coming from us; our competence is from God, who has made us
competent to be ministers of a new covenant, not of letter but of spirit;
for the letter kills, but the Spirit gives life.*

2 CORINTHIANS 3:4-6

*It is part of the discipline of humility that we must not spare our hand
where it can perform a service and that we do not assume that our
schedule is our own to manage, but allow it to be arranged by God.*

DIETRICH BONHOEFFER, *LIFE TOGETHER*

*Yet another elder said: If you see a young monk by his own will
climbing up into heaven, take him by the foot and throw him to the
ground, because what he is doing is not good for him.*

THOMAS MERTON, *THE WISDOM OF THE DESERT*

"Wherever Thou leadest, I will follow."

ROBERT DUVALL IN *THE APOSTLE*

SPIRITUAL POWER FLOWED THROUGH Paul's ministry, but Paul is clear that it didn't come from him. He is a channel, a vessel, a mere conductor of the Spirit's life-giving power that flows through him and his ministry. In the passage from 2 Corinthians cited above Paul applies this to all of us with his use of "we." What is true for Paul, for his coworkers and for the Corinthians is true for all Christians including, you and me[1]: "Not that we are competent of ourselves to claim anything as coming from us; our competence is from God" (2 Cor 3:5).

To experience empowered leadership we first have to learn Who is the source of the power, that true power does not come from ourselves, or our efforts or our human wisdom. "We have this treasure in clay jars, so that it may be made clear that this extraordinary power belongs to God and does not come from us" (2 Cor 4:7). Then we have to be fashioned by God into conduits of this power. God is the one who equips and empowers effective ministry. Effective ministry is the kind of ministry that bestows life in the Spirit on others and gives a foretaste of the kingdom of God come in fullness. God is the one who gives life, through Jesus, by the Spirit: "our competence is from God, who has made us competent to be ministers of a new covenant, not of letter but of spirit; for the letter kills, but the Spirit gives life" (2 Cor 3:6).

Followership

Since this is true, what we need are not new pioneers and trailblazers to lead us into the future. What we need are yielded followers who are conduits of the Spirit's power to bring people into the presence and kingdom of God. We need leaders who model how to submit to God and receive God's strength and cleansing for service in the world. It is exciting to feel strong, competent and in charge, but there is no true spiritual power in this, no ability to materialize God's kingdom reality. Life-giving leadership flows from a deep dependency on the One who empowers, cleanses, guides and gives life.

In short, what we need is followership, not leadership. The leaders we need must model how to follow after Christ, to live under Christ's rule, to become more like Jesus in trusting dependency upon God. Any Tom, Dick or Sally can come up with an idea and get others to start building the building, growing the group, planning the program or gathering up the money. There is nothing essentially Christian about these things. Churches are not the only ones who do this—so do corporations and cults. If this is leadership, then we have had enough of it in the church. Too often these so-called leaders model more materialism, more life "according to the flesh." We will come back to this point again later.

Paul modeled followership. I don't think I even noticed this about Paul's ministry until I made the quantum leap in my ministry from planning to following. Don't get me wrong. I am not now talking against being organized, against being a careful steward of time or against coordinating the efforts of various teams to accomplish an agreed upon end. Instead I am talking against a manner of ministry that is based on human control and direction rather than God's leading and empowerment. I am trying to shine a light on the lie being hawked in seminars and seminaries that "ministry means management."

We have to face the facts. The description of events in Acts is not that Paul was the master visionary who laid out a fifteen-year plan to evangelize major centers in the Roman Empire, who would in turn evangelize their regions.[2] He was not a leader in that sense of being a visionary. Instead we see a stop-and-start picture of Paul's ministry interrupted by human opposition and often redirected by the Spirit's guidance. For example, Paul was just getting started in Thessalonica when a riot drove him out of town (Acts 17:1-10). If you asked any church-planting expert today, there is no way one could plant a church in just three or four weeks that will survive for the long haul. And yet that is exactly what Paul did. He writes back to the Thessalonians as though they are a fully functioning Christian community, "to the church in Thessalonica" (1 Thess 1:1; 2 Thess 2:1). When God wants to accomplish something through us, following—not planning—is what is needed.

"The first two words of sound Christian theology," said my mentor F. Dale Bruner, "are *God can.*" Once we understand this, we can understand the whole of theology and develop a faith built on a solid foundation. God is able. God doesn't need Noah or Moses to understand or make sense of the ark or the exodus. God merely requires their obedience. The rain did come, and the sea did part. God can. Similar powerful acts can take place when we too are in alignment with what God has chosen to do.

This is what the leaders of the early church in Antioch understood. God is able. They did not need a plan. They needed to know the mind of God through the Spirit. This was normal Christian leadership of Paul's day:

> While they were worshiping the Lord and fasting, the Holy Spirit said, "Set apart for me Barnabas and Saul for the work to which I have called them." . . . So, being sent out by the Holy Spirit, they went down to Seleucia; and from there they sailed to Cyprus. When they arrived at Salamis, they proclaimed the word of God. (Acts 13:2, 4-5)

Spirit-led, Spirit-inspired, Spirit-empowered—they obeyed God, and their leadership was life giving. The text does not tell us how they heard, but that the Holy Spirit spoke to them while they were praying and fasting. Presumably this word came through one of their prophets. The direction explicitly did not come from a visionary leader. The results speak for themselves. The love of Jesus was spread throughout the

Roman Empire, and mission-station churches were established in strategic locations for the furtherance of the gospel.

The left-brain rationalist (LBR) inside of me is objecting now (is your LBR objecting too?). What about all the lunatics who claim to be led by God and lead people astray? What about all the irresponsible people who blame God for things they do? Can't you imagine how messy this could make things? How are we going to guard against abuses of authority? What about the lunatic fringe who take things like this and use them to wreak havoc in a church? (My LBR continues to shout objections as I fade back to ponder this passage of Scripture.) The truth is that a vision that comes from a leader's self-will and is imposed on other Christians is just as destructive and oppressive. The Reformation principle should be applied here: the abuse of a thing never nullifies its proper use. That people abuse claims of being led by the Spirit does not mean we should neglect to be led by the Spirit ourselves.

The real issue is not our rational objections but our obsessive need to maintain a high sense of control. As Mike Yaconelli aptly says in *Dangerous Wonder,*

> But truth is unpredictable when Jesus is present; everyone is uncomfortable yet mysteriously glad at the same time. People do not like surprises—even church people—and they don't want to be uncomfortable. They want a nice, tame Jesus. You know what? Tameness is not an option. Take surprise out of faith and all that is left is dry and dead religion.[3]

Instead of rationalizations, I want to respond to my LBR with an obvious biblical observation. This is what Scripture says happened—they were led by the Spirit. We must do the math and couple this with the fruit: the Spirit moved in power through their ministry. Spirit-led ministers release Spirit-power in their ministry. Life is spread forth.

I can multiply examples. Paul was eager to preach the gospel everywhere, but at one point during his second missionary journey, he ministered in Phrygia and Galatia because he had been "forbidden by the Holy Spirit to speak the word in Asia" (Acts 16:6). Why? God had that base covered? Someone else was being sent there? The timing was wrong? Who knows! Later, on his third journey, he would cut through Colossae and Ephesus on his way to Troas. But this time he had to do a lengthy end run to the north: "When they came opposite Mysia, they attempted to go into Bithynia, but the Spirit of Jesus did not allow them; so, passing by Mysia, they went down to Troas" (Acts 16:7).

Following, not planning. That is what Paul's leadership and ministry were about. He obeyed, and the night they arrived in Troas Paul found out why the Spirit had directed him in this manner. God planned to use him and his companions to spread the message about Jesus and start mission-station churches throughout Macedonia, the province where Philippi, Thessalonica, Apollonia and Berea are located. "During the night Paul had a vision: there stood a man of Macedonia pleading with him and saying, 'Come over to Macedonia and help us.' When he had seen the vision, we immediately tried to cross over to Macedonia, being convinced that God had called us to proclaim the good news to them" (Acts 16:9-10).

And so the gospel was spread and the church was established along the eastern edge of Macedonia, and even down to Athens and across to Corinth in just a few short months. Nobody planned it. They were following the guidance of the Holy Spirit. God beckoned—and they followed. By navigating from God's revealed will, they were positioned right where they needed to be. If they had stuck to a preconceived blueprint, they would have missed what God was doing.

Later the Holy Spirit directs Paul to Jerusalem, the least likely place he—or we, under the circumstances—would plan to go. With the opposition and plots against his life, why would he head to Jerusalem? No reason at all; that is why Luke reports Paul's sense of being compelled by the Spirit: "And now, as a captive to the Spirit, I am on my way to Jerusalem, not knowing what will happen to me there, except that the Holy Spirit testifies to me in every city that imprisonment and persecutions are waiting for me" (Acts 20:22-23).

Paul had to be dragged there. We might say, following the Spirit in this case led in the opposite direction anyone with common sense would have planned to go. Yet the fruit of Paul's obedience is evident for all to see. We have the benefit of twenty-twenty hindsight, and we can see that Paul made it safely there, then on to Rome, and presumably on to the western edge of the Empire in Spain. Planning did not point him there. Following the Spirit did.

We should let this fully sink in. We cannot dismiss this as "the way they did things back then, in that different culture." We should be aware that this was just as troubling for many LBRs then as it is for us now. The Corinthians, for example, were perplexed when Paul changed plans because when he "came to Troas to proclaim the good news of Christ, a door was opened for me in the Lord" (2 Cor 2:12; see 2 Cor 1:15 – 2:13 for the full account). The Corinthians were bothered by this, and many of us would have been too. "You didn't come, Paul, like you planned? You were following the Spirit? What kind of explanation is that?" Yet there it is. That's Paul's explanation.

But that is not all. Paul calls us to follow his example: "If we live by the Spirit, let us also be guided by the Spirit" (Gal 5:25). That is how the NRSV translates it, but "guided" is far too weak of a word to do justice to the strong Greek *stoichōmen*, whose origin is in the military terminology of obedient alignment.[4] This does not mean "take the Spirit's guidance under advisement." To be in accord with the Spirit is to submit to God's mind and purpose on the matter, to do what the Spirit says should be done, to be "led by the Spirit" (Gal 5:17). Perhaps the natural rendering of this verse made the translators, like us, queasy? The sense should be, "If we live by the Spirit, let us also be controlled by the Spirit." That's what Paul kept modeling, and it is clear what he means by it. This is not the raving of a charismaniac. This is what the Scriptures say.

But what if this hasn't been your experience of God? What if this kind of personal interaction through the Holy Spirit has been missing from your life? I'm guessing this also means that you haven't experienced an empowered ministry. You may have experienced results, but were they life-giving results? Was the kingdom multiplied? Were people transformed into New Testament Christians and sent out to not-yet Christians? Did Jesus Christ become the center of their lives, or were the results that your church or ministry became the center of their lives?

How do you move from powerless planning to empowered following? There is a simple answer and a complicated answer to this question. The simple answer is, we ask God to lead us, and we go where we are led and do what we are told. The complicated answer is that we have to cut free from the forces inside us and outside us that lead us astray and keep us from hearing and obeying God's direction. The internal force we need to be freed from Paul calls the "flesh"; the external force Paul calls people pleasing. The remainder of this chapter is about how we move over to Spirit-led, Spirit-empowered, life-giving ministry.

Living and Leading "According to the Spirit" Versus "According to the Flesh"

"Flesh" (Greek *sarx*) is a challenging but crucial term to understand Paul's theology and to understand the path to empowered leadership. "Flesh" is not the same as "body" but overlaps a little in usage and meaning. "Flesh" is a negative term in Paul, whereas "body" is neutral: flesh ≠ body. The two overlap but are not synonymous.[5]

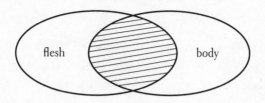

Figure 2.1. The overlap in meaning of *flesh* and *body*

The usage of "flesh" that is crucial for understanding this chapter has to do with living "according to the flesh" (Greek *kata sarka*) in contrast to life lived "according to the Spirit" *(kata pneuma)*. The problem with people living "according to the flesh" is they are not submitted to God's will and God's way. The problem with "flesh" is a problem with the will, with sinful and rebellious willfulness toward God's rule. "Flesh" is not about living "in the body" but about the spiritual condition of willful independence from God and God's will. It is more than physical temptations (as "carnal" might imply, the older word used to translate *sarx*). Perhaps the best way to define "flesh" in this sense is self-will or independent willfulness—a person in the spiritual condition of standing aloof from God and what God wants that person to be and do.[6]

There are two key passages in Paul for us to dig into to understand the difference between living "according to the flesh" and living "according to the Spirit." The first of these is Romans 8:5-9:

For those who live according to the flesh set their minds on the things of the flesh, but those who live according to the Spirit set their minds on the things of the Spirit. To set the mind on the flesh is death, but to set the mind on the Spirit is life and peace. For this reason the mind that is set on the flesh is hostile to God; it does not submit to God's law—indeed it cannot, and those who are in the flesh cannot please God. But you are not in the flesh; you are in the Spirit, since the Spirit

*of God dwells in you. Anyone who does not have the Spirit of Christ
does not belong to him.*

Paul lays out a sharp contradiction between two ways to live. The first
of these is "according to the flesh." Those who live according to the flesh
are often not aware of it, but the direction they are heading is toward disappointment, destruction, "death." I am convinced many Christian
leaders are leading by the flesh and are unaware of it. This flesh/death
equation mirrors the wisdom of the Old Testament: "There is a way that
seems right to a person, but its end is the way to death" (Prov 14:12). Not
only does it eventually lead to dire consequences, but also it is a way of
living that continually offends God, is "hostile to God." Why is living
"according to the flesh" antagonistic to God? Because those who live as
such do not submit to what God wants, nor are they able (v. 7). They
cannot "please God" or hope to see God's favor because they are treacherous, living under another kingdom and monarch, the kingdom of "I."
Submission to God is the key, and many never find life-giving ministry
because they refuse to submit.

Whoever surrenders the "kingdom of I" to God has submitted to the
lordship of Jesus and receives the love and blessing of the gift of the
Holy Spirit (Rom 8:5). When we receive God's gift of the Spirit we experience the blessings of living under God's rule: life in place of death,
and peace in place of enmity with God (Rom 8:7). Anyone who is a
Christian, anyone who has submitted to a trusting relationship with
God through Jesus Christ, has the Spirit dwelling in him or her. "Anyone who does not have the Spirit of Christ does not belong to him"
(Rom 8:9). Paul states that being a Christian is the same as being Spirit-
filled. To be a Christian leader is the same as being a Spirit-filled leader.
The only other option Paul leaves open is life "according to the flesh" —
and he makes clear where that leads.

As a leader, I have lived out both flesh-controlled and Spirit-led ministry. The difference is as dramatic as the distinction between rowing and sailing. A rower gets to a destination by personal strain, struggle and effort. A sailor arrives under the wind's power. Rowing is a good way to keep in shape but a lousy way to travel. Sailing taps the power of the wind and allows us to go much farther, much faster, with far less human effort than rowing. For too many years I ministered like rowing a boat: out of my strength, in my wisdom, by my power. I preached and taught out of my good ideas, scripturally based though most all of them were. At the time it didn't seem so, but I was in effect a Christian Pharisee. I believed and taught the Bible, but there was no power flowing through my ministry (that is not to say God didn't use my ministry—he did, since his Word accomplishes amazing things in spite of the messenger). Since then, I have been learning the difference between preaching and teaching biblically "according to the flesh" and preaching biblically and powerfully "according to the Spirit." Sailing is a far better way to go. The rest of this book is an attempt to describe in detail how to stay on the high road of ministry by the Spirit and off the low road of ministry "according to your flesh."

Passing Over to the Path of Power: Self-Surrender

Self-surrender is how we cut free from the cords of the "flesh." The problem of the flesh can be illustrated by an image of driving a car. When we live according to the flesh, we have our hands wrapped with white knuckles on the controls of our lives and therefore our families and our ministries. Self-surrender is releasing our grip on the directional controls and sliding into the assistant driver seat, allowing God to fully occupy the driver's seat and control the steering wheel. We participate in the journey as God asks and requires us, and we do not countermand what God wants.

Some Christians are almost surrendered, what we might call an "almost Christian."[7] But whenever a crucial issue surfaces involving their career, their finances or their future, they lean over and grab the wheel or cram their foot on the brake. They replace obedience and submission to God with the arrogance of self-will and determination. Whenever I think of this, I think of a two-year-old yelling, "I can do it all by myself." This willful stance shuts down the Spirit's power in their lives, and it is like turning off the keys in the ignition. The "flesh" takes control, and the Spirit's power is dissipated. It is not that God is not present but that the Spirit refuses to pour out power in this circumstance.

Why is that? I picture it like this. When my daughter was ten years old she really liked to talk about and think about driving, but she did not yet have the physical size or foresight to take on this major responsibility. I refused to let her take the wheel. Imagine us driving down the road. If she grabbed the steering wheel or stabbed at the brakes with her foot, we would be in big trouble! If she were able to force me out of the driver's seat, I would make every effort to turn off the power before she got control. Power requires responsibility. In the case of spiritual leaders, responsibility comes when we have humbled ourselves and admitted that we cannot do God's job of long-term planning and directional steering to bring in the fullness of the kingdom.

Instead, we are like ten-year-olds wanting to drive when we so confidently assert a direction for ourselves or our ministries without any prompting or direction from God. God's heavenly authority and capacity are more than we can handle. We are like ten-year-olds when it comes to the future and when it comes to knowing the mind of God for the future. We know bits and pieces, as God has revealed them in Scripture. But none of us can see clearly where each road leads, what obstacles and opposition lie ahead and what path leads us all the way to our heavenly home. None of us except God, that is. That is why self-surrender is more sensible than self-determination and why God empowers only those who are yielded.

Many or most of us probably do not come to a place of surrender and yielding on our own. Paul didn't. He was on the road to death, but he was thoroughly convinced he was serving God—on his way to murder Christians in Damascus, with the approval of his religious superiors! That is when the risen Jesus confronted him, knocked him to his knees and blinded him. Paul's physical blindness ironically became the beginning of his awakening to life in the Spirit, when he received true spiritual sight. It came as a lightning bolt out of the blue for Paul, and it was quite a shock for the first Christians to meet this changed man (see Acts 9:1-31; 22:1-21; 26:1-23). He was transformed from death to life, from flesh living to Spirit-led living for Jesus, in a moment of crushing, submission and surrender. In a moment he had to give up all he once held dear, everything he had built his life upon to that point. This brings us to the other important passage we need to read closely, Philippians 3:3-11.

In Philippians 3, Paul warns his dear friends about pseudo-missionaries traveling around insisting that Gentile Christians must be circumcised. In Galatians he calls these troublemakers "Judaizers," since they insisted on Gentiles being circumcised and observing dietary restrictions and the Jewish holy calendar.[8] In warning his friends at Philippi about these people, Paul explains clearly what had changed for him when he bowed his will to Jesus in yielded submission:

> For it is we who are the circumcision, who worship in the Spirit of God and boast in Christ Jesus and have no confidence in the flesh—even though I, too, have reason for confidence in the flesh.
>
> If anyone else has reason to be confident in the flesh, I have more: circumcised on the eighth day, a member of the people of Israel, of the tribe of Benjamin, a Hebrew born of Hebrews; as to the law, a Pharisee; as to zeal, a persecutor of the church; as to righteousness under the law, blameless.

Yet whatever gains I had, these I have come to regard as loss because
of Christ. More than that, I regard everything as loss because of the
surpassing value of knowing Christ Jesus my Lord. For his sake I have
suffered the loss of all things, and I regard them as rubbish, in order
that I may gain Christ and be found in him, not having a righteous-
ness of my own that comes from the law, but one that comes through
faith in Christ, the righteousness from God based on faith. I want to
know Christ and the power of his resurrection and the sharing of his
sufferings by becoming like him in his death, if somehow I may attain
the resurrection from the dead. (Phil 3:3-11)

Here the contrast is the same as Romans 8, but Paul distinguishes
the attitude of confidence "in the flesh" and what it means to be "in
Christ." Paul identifies "confidence in the flesh" as confidence in religious ceremonies (circumcision), confidence in his lineage and
elite family and social connections (Israelite, tribe of Benjamin, "Hebrew of Hebrews"), confidence in his efforts at perfectionism as a
Pharisee ("blameless") and confidence in his zeal (as a persecutor of
Christians). By the world's standards, at least by the standard of self-
respecting Jews of his day, Paul had every reason for confidence "in
the flesh" (Phil 3:4).

This confidence was misplaced. It was confidence in human
achievement and not in God. When he met Jesus, literally face to face,
on the road to Damascus, he cashed in these confidence chips. When
he compared them with his new experience of life "in Jesus," he realized they were *skybala*, a very rude word that the NRSV and NIV deli-
cately translate "rubbish" (the King James Version is closer with "dung";
Phil 3:8). He came to realize all these things that he once esteemed
were now repugnant compared with this superior treasure of life in
Jesus, life lived according to the Spirit of Jesus. He became passionate

about life that is found in Jesus: "I want to know Christ and the power of his resurrection and the sharing of his sufferings by becoming like him in his death, if somehow I may attain the resurrection from the dead" (Phil 3:10). His message became, "Sell all, and buy Christ! Renounce all self-confidence and willful self-determination, and yield and surrender to the will and purpose of God in Jesus Christ!"

For most of us passing over from willfulness "in the flesh" to the place of yieldedness to Christ is more of process than a one-time event. We begin by moving from a place of pride toward humility. (I am using "pride" in the negative sense similar to "in the flesh," not the positive sense of healthy self-esteem.) "Pride goes before destruction, and a haughty spirit before a fall. It is better to be of a lowly spirit among the poor than to divide the spoil with the proud" (Prov 16:18-19). God opposes prideful "in the flesh" living but honors the humble.

Let me try to illustrate this process of moving over from life in the flesh to life in the Spirit. In figure 2.2, the check mark on the line represents where I am on the scale of "proud" to "not very proud." I'm not as proud, as "fleshly," as I used to be. I'm moving on to "not very proud." In fact, I may even be proud that I am "not very proud," and this indicates I have a way to go.

proud   not very proud

Figure 2.2. The proud/not very proud scale

Humbling events and humiliating circumstances come along, and my perspective is then broadened considerably. I realize I need to grow

quite a bit more. I have made some strides away from pride, but I find
that "not very proud" is still a state of pride, of egotism, of the "flesh." I
have been humbled enough to see that I have a way to go. I'm "not very
proud," but I'm still too concerned with what others think of me, still
too bothered by the offenses and slights I encounter, still too absorbed
with weighing my blessings and trials with what others receive. I am still
in a state of powerlessness for ministry. I have not passed over the crucial
boundary from Dodd to God, from self-will to God's marvelous empowerment (see figure 2.3)

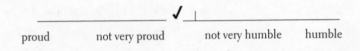

proud   not very proud   not very humble   humble

Figure 2.3. Still short of empowered ministry

In figure 2.2, the divider in the middle marks the boundary point between powerlessness and power in the Spirit. It also coincides with living a self-willed life, according to the flesh, on the left, and living a
surrendered, Spirit-empowered life, on the right. I pass over from one
to the other when I surrender my will, my future, my self-determination
to God (see figure 2.3). The more I yield myself to God's direction and
control (the further I move to the right), the more power is released in
my ministry and life. We are entrusted with this treasure when we have
learned not to grab the steering wheel. Greater power requires greater
self-restraint. Self-surrender is the path to the Spirit's power, experiencing and being enabled by the power that comes from God.

Most of us probably don't participate in the process voluntarily. The
renowned London preacher of the nineteenth century, Charles Spurgeon, aptly puts it this way: God dashes us to pieces before he exalts us.

He says, "Is it not a curious thing that, whenever God means to make a man great, He always breaks him in pieces first?"[9] This is the example

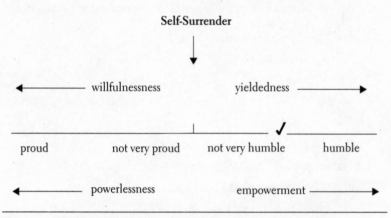

Figure 2.4. Empowered ministry

of Jesus and his followers and the witness of the spiritual greats who have walked the face of the earth. To yield to God's purposes, we must have our wills broken and tamed. Spurgeon continues:

> Have none of you ever noticed, in your own lives, that whenever God is going to give you an enlargement, and bring you out to a larger sphere of service, or a higher platform of spiritual life, you always get thrown down? That is His usual way of working; He makes you hungry before He feeds you; He strips you before He robes you; He makes nothing of you before He makes something of you. This was the way with David. He is to be king in Jerusalem; but he must go to the throne by the way of the cave. Now, are any of you here going to heaven, or going to a more heavenly state of sanctification, or going to a greater sphere of usefulness: Do not wonder if you go by the way of the cave.[10]

When we know the depth of our need for God and are convinced that God's purpose is far superior to our preferences, then we are ready to yield to God. The process is painful and often unwanted, but it is necessary to pass over to the path of empowered ministry by the Spirit.

> I asked God for strength, that I might achieve,
> I was made weak, that I might learn humbly to obey.
> I asked for health, that I might do greater things,
> I was given infirmity, that I might do better things.
> I asked for riches, that I might be happy,
> I was given poverty, that I might be wise.
> I asked for power, that I might have the praise of men,
> I was given weakness, that I might feel the need of God.
> I asked for all things, that I might enjoy life,
> I was given life, that I might enjoy all things.
> I got nothing that I asked for, but everything I had hoped for.
> Almost despite myself, my unspoken prayers were answered.
> I am among men most richly blessed.
> —Author Unknown

Doing What God Wants Done: Brokenness

When we cross over from self-willed existence to yieldedness to the Lord, we now put ourselves in a continual position of readiness to do what God wants us to do. The Christian secret to a happy life, and the most crucial characteristic for a life-giving leader is the same thing: doing what God wants done. We can choose to obey God faithfully and radically and make it a habit of our lives. Or, many of us have to be conditioned to obedience through a spiritual process of breaking. To get there by our choice, we must be convinced that humanly conceived plans and initiatives bring death not life. Probably not many of us get to that place by our choice. Too often we must experience deep brokenness and despair over our efforts before we are truly open to seeking and doing God's will alone.

You could say we need to be broken, much like a horse needs to be broken to be useful. Imagine God as the rider and yourself as the horse. If you are broken, you are at the Master's command. When you are broken, the divine Rider can easily steer you at higher and higher speeds, without any apprehension that you will turn left into a ditch when the rein nudges you to the right onto a path only the Lord can see. Surrender increases our trustworthiness, and so our Master entrusts us with more authority, more power. The only people he doesn't give power to are those who are looking for power rather than submitting to his intended purpose for the power: reconciling the world gone wrong to himself.

When we habitually seek out first and only God's will, a flow and an ease come to our ministry. There is no need to force things. Force is the way of the flesh. Instead, often doors will open easily and barriers fall at the touch of the feather when we are following God's direction. The doors the Lord opens no one can close, and nothing can stop God's forward movement. Those who are directed by the Spirit can be effective and gentle, because they don't need to force any doors open (see Col 3:12; 1 Thess 2:7; 2 Tim 2:24).

When we are living and leading "in the flesh," we have to force things. The path has not been cleared for us, and we carry the weight of responsibility without God's help. We strain, we press, we grind it out. We are pulling a two-horse plow as a solo horse, and the most formidable harness is empty: we don't have God's shoulder pulling with us.

The first thing that a lot of leaders "in the flesh" need to learn is that God is already up to something. When we get our pride and our need to take credit out of the way, we can see that God is already at work, doing something that we can join him in. Theologically, this is called prevenient grace. God is already at work. When we put our shoulder to that plow, the divine Partner pulls most of the weight and the work flows and is blessed.

This is what empowered leadership is. The psalmist knew this truth: "Unless the LORD builds the house, / those who build it labor in vain. / Unless the LORD guards the city, / the guard keeps watch in vain" (Ps 127:1).

Often times we are frustrated in our witnessing and evangelism efforts for this very reason. We determine to go take God to someone, rather than discerning which fields are ripe for harvest and joining in what God is doing. I lead an evangelism equipping ministry called Share Jesus! in which we equip churches and disciples to be more effective witnesses. One of the most important things we teach them about evangelism is this: whenever you walk into a room or a park or a party, pray "Lord, show me who to stand next to," and then follow the prompting of the Holy Spirit. This takes all of the anxiety out of the process. We are not taking God to that person, but we are joining God in what grace is already doing in that person's life. I have seen people do this and lead someone to Christ and into the church within a matter of minutes. Does that sound far-fetched? This is exactly what happened with Phillip and the Ethiopian eunuch (Acts 8:26-40).[11]

Of course, with all of this I am assuming that God's written will revealed in Scripture is the guardrail on the road we travel. Spirit-given direction can tell us what road to take but will never ask us to pass through the ethical guardrail of God's written Word to us in the Bible. Spirit-led living is not in place of biblically informed thinking and deciding but complementary to it, a both-and rather than an either-or. The point is rather that willfulness, rebellion and stubborn independence from God are a sieve in our souls where no divine power can be contained. Surrender, yieldedness, humility, brokenness, cleansing, trust and obedience cup our souls to receive and disperse the power God pours out on the humble and humbled. "We have this treasure in clay jars, so that it may be made clear that this extraordinary power belongs to God and does not come from us" (2 Cor 4:7).

Freedom in Slavery: The Power Is the Master's

For those of us from the individualistic and permissive West, all this talk of surrender, submission and radical obedience may grate on our tastes. We tend to be have-our-cake-and-eat-it-too Christians, envisioning the kingdom of God to be something like the government of Great Britain. Jesus is king with all the pomp and circumstance and worship that entails. But I am prime minister, with all the real authority to make policy and decisions. Jesus is the figurehead king who ratifies my decisions and rescues me from difficulties. But I call the shots and have charge of my staff, my time and my money. This is living "in the flesh" when we wrongly think we are living "according to the Spirit."

When Paul pays honor again and again to Jesus as Lord (*kyrios*), it is clear that he often understands this term in its common usage of a master who owns and controls slaves.[12] Paul understands his role as Christ's slave (*doulos*), who is compelled and controlled by his master to do the master's bidding and to serve his purposes. It is common knowledge among readers of the Greek New Testament that English translations of the Bible have subtly covered up the images of slavery in the New Testament. Translations tend to use the more socially acceptable term "servant" instead of "slave" in translating the some 190 words in the New Testament associated with slavery, without a doubt because of our collective shame over our history of chattel slavery. Scholars know that awareness of the master-slave imagery is crucial to understanding Paul's letters today as they would have been perceived in the first century. The practice of slavery was prevalent, the very economic foundation of the Roman Empire. It is estimated that one-third of the Roman Empire at the time of Paul would have been slaves, one-third masters and another one-third former slaves who had been emancipated.[13]

One of Paul's most common self-characterizations is "slave of Christ." Since our English translations tend to gloss over this fact, it is worthwhile to cite some of the many instances of Paul's self-portrayal as Christ's slave. He introduces himself to the Romans as "Paul, a slave of Christ Jesus, a called apostle, set apart for the gospel of God" (Rom 1:1). It is common to designate Paul as an apostle and think of that as his most common self-portrait. But this verse hints at what was a social convention: "apostles," emissaries, that is, were usually slaves serving as their masters' representatives. In Romans 1:1 "apostle" is mentioned second in line after "slave." To the Philippians he introduces himself and Timothy simply as "slaves of Christ Jesus" (Phil 1:1). Obviously Paul had communicated his understanding of enslaved leadership to his star pupil, Timothy (see 2 Tim 2:24). Epaphras had this same training from his mentor, Paul (Col 4:12).

Paul makes it clear that using the image of slavery to understand one's relationship with Christ has to do with obedience. For Paul, the issue is black and white: everybody obeys something, and whatever or whomever you obey, you are enslaved to. In different language, he contrasts the flesh-Christ tension we discussed above as "slavery to sin" versus "slavery to righteousness" (Rom 6:16; cf. Gal 4:3). When we have been set free from slavery to sin, we "serve as slaves to God" (Rom 6:22). In 1 Corinthians, anyone who is a Christian ("in Christ") has become "a slave of Christ" (1 Cor 7:22). Paul says he himself is one such person, not a slave in society's eyes (*eleutheros*, "free"), but he serves as God's slave for all people (1 Cor 9:19). This is how Paul summarizes his message as obedience to the Master, Jesus: "For we do not proclaim ourselves but Jesus Christ as Lord (*kyrios*), and ourselves as your slaves (*douloi*) on account of Jesus" (2 Cor 4:5).

Paul simply follows in the steps of Jesus, who humbled himself and took on "the form of a slave" (Phil 2:7). This was reflective of Jesus' pattern of leadership that he set for the first disciples. John's Gospel narrates one instance when Jesus specifically modeled slavelike leadership. It was as difficult for those disciples as it is for us to think of the Christian leadership role like that of the lowest slave. The whole scene was awkward for them, which Peter's reaction makes obvious.

> *And during supper Jesus, knowing that the Father had given all things into his hands, and that he had come from God and was going to God, got up from the table, took off his outer robe, and tied a towel around himself. Then he poured water into a basin and began to wash the disciples' feet and to wipe them with the towel that was tied around him. He came to Simon Peter, who said to him, "Lord, are you going to wash my feet?" Jesus answered, "You do not know now what I am doing, but later you will understand." Peter said to him, "You will never wash my feet." Jesus answered, "Unless I wash you, you have no share with me." Simon Peter said to him, "Lord, not my feet only but also my hands and my head!" Jesus said to him, "One who has bathed does not need to wash, except for the feet, but is entirely clean. And you are clean, though not all of you." For he knew who was to betray him; for this reason he said, "Not all of you are clean." (Jn 13:2-11)*

Jesus goes on to explicitly call them "slaves" of their "master" and teacher, Jesus, who has modeled for them what enslaved, empowered leadership is supposed to look like.

> *After he had washed their feet, had put on his robe, and had returned to the table, he said to them, "Do you know what I have done to you? You call me Teacher and Lord—and you are right, for that is what I am. So if I, your Lord and Teacher, have washed your feet, you also ought to wash one another's feet. For I have set you an example, that you also should do as I have done to you. Very truly, I tell you, servants [douloi, "slaves"] are not greater than their master, nor are messengers greater than the one who sent them. If you know these things, you are blessed if you do them. (Jn 13:12-17)*

Jesus and Paul make it clear that Christian leadership is best characterized as slavery to the Master, Jesus, with all that it implies: submission
and obedience. This is another way of saying the power comes from the
One who directs our lives and our leadership. Empowerment is found
in the liberating enslavement to Jesus as Lord. In that choice of submission and obedience we are freed from the unseen master pulling our
chain: the "flesh," the sinful side of ourselves, "sin." Everyone serves
one master or the other (Rom 6:16).

We Cannot Serve Two Masters:
The Problem with People Pleasing

There is another form of life "according to the flesh" that every leader
must confront: the pressure to be a people pleaser. We all know leaders
who pander to the polls, who knuckle under to pressure, who take the
path of least resistance, who seek to avoid conflict and keep everybody
happy. Their ministries are never empowered ministries, and in the end
they fail to keep everybody happy. When it is time to make a decision,
they are found with their finger in the air, testing the winds of public
opinion. The result of people pleasing is that the outspoken minority
controls the ministry or church on the "squeaky wheel gets the grease"
principle. In reality, the collective flesh of griping people is the tail that
wags the dog. A leader's ego-need for approval submarines the godly
leader's responsibility to focus on God's will and God's glory. There is a
way that seems right to a person, but it leads to destruction . . .

In a revealing confrontation with the Galatian church, Paul succinctly sets his example for them to compare themselves against: "For
now am I seeking to please people or God? If I were still seeking to
please people, I would not be Christ's slave" (Gal 1:10). The Galatian
Christians were feeling the pressure of interlopers to accept the necessity of circumcision for their salvation. Paul must have discerned the im-

mense pressure being brought to bear on them, because he makes resistance to people pleasing one of the main issues of his multipronged argument (in addition to demonstrating theologically that they did not need to be circumcised).[14] By this pithy "I" statement, he sets a clear example for them to stay true to their Lord and master and to reject this other master of public pressure and opinion.

Galatians 1:10, in my mind, explains why Paul goes on to recount his public confrontation with Peter (Gal 2:11-15). He is modeling for the Galatians how to stand firm against the pressure of influential people. Peter shamefully caved in to people pressure. Paul does all he can to convince the Galatians not to do what Peter did, not to succumb to those who wanted them to be circumcised and observe dietary restrictions in order to be saved (Gal 2:14).

It is amazing how much unconscious pressure we can feel from other people to act or decide one way or another. When a leader of a ministry is a people pleaser, the results are devastating. They are no longer "led by the Spirit" but are led by public opinion, the flesh writ large. This may appear democratic or participatory in their style, but often this means the squeaky wheel of someone's flesh gets the grease—and the rest of the body gets the shaft! How much more pernicious, how much more devious and destructive when the leader consciously panders to power players or moneyed people.

The story is told of a college experiment in which a control group was brought in on a deception. They were told that when two sticks were held up before them, all of them together were to say that the clearly shorter stick was the longest. This was not a study in measurement but peer pressure. One after another, subjects were brought in. When asked to vote on the longest stick, they would consistently label the shorter stick as the longer, assuming "this large a group must be right." The power of people pleasing to deceive and misdirect is obvious.

The same thing happens with worse results in a church. People pleasers avoid confrontation because they want to make people happy, avoid conflict and keep things running smoothly. In fact, it is a good thing to maintain unity in the body of Christ. But unity at the price of pleasing people instead of pleasing God is no unity. God is not pleased, and the power of the Holy Spirit is never evident in such circumstances. People pleasing becomes downright demonic when the leader is on a career track, pleasing people to promote himself or herself or avoiding conflict "to keep my job." No wonder so many of us have experienced deep darkness in the church. In fear the shepherd on watch lets the wolves run freely among the sheep.

Frankly, people pleasing is never loving if the hard word is what is needed. If I have a cancerous tumor, and you tell me everything is okay, you have been cruel and heartless. The loving thing to do is to let me know what the problem is so I can address it, attack it, do something about it while I can. "Ignorance is bliss" but guarantees that the tumor will eat my lunch.

The pressure to please people instead of obey God is implicit in this humorous code of "How to Rate a Sermon." Implicit here is the high cost, sometimes, of standing by the truth rather than seeking to make people happy by what we say.

How to Rate a Sermon

"G"   Generally acceptable to everyone. Full of inoffensive, puerile platitudes; usually described as "wonderful" or "marvelous."

"PG" For more mature congregations. At times this sermon even makes the gospel relevant to today's issues; may even contain mild suggestions for change. Often described as "challenging" or "thought provoking," even though no one intends to take any action or change any attitude.

"R" Definitely restricted to those not upset by the truth. This sermon tells it like it is. Threatening to the comfortable; most often described as "disturbing" or "controversial." Usually indicates that the preacher has an outside source of income.

"X" Positively limited to those who can handle explosive ideas. This sermon really socks it to 'em. It is the kind of sermon that landed Jeremiah in the well, got Amos run out of town, set things up for the stoning of Stephen; always described as "shocking" or "in poor taste." The minister who preaches this sermon had better have his suitcase packed and his life insurance paid up.

Sometimes it is difficult for caring pastors to keep a balance between serving people and pleasing them. Bob Schaper, a seminary professor of mine, taught me a motto that has helped me keep the balance between obedience to Christ and a servantlike posture towards people: *I am your servant, but you are not my master.*

This reminder has helped me maintain a servant stance, even when dealing with the power brokers that we too often find in leadership positions in church. It is liberating to realize that I am free in Christ to serve you, even if you demand it of me. One thing I keep clear: I take my marching orders from a single Master. Yet I maintain complete submission to the Lord Jesus by maintaining a servant stance toward others.

Paul's self-description of his stance toward flattery is our model for dealing with the treacherous problem of people pleasing:

Just as we have been approved by God to be entrusted with the message of the gospel, even so we speak, not to please mortals, but to please God who tests our hearts. As you know and as God is our witness, we never came with words of flattery or with a pretext for greed; nor did we seek praise from mortals, whether from you or from others. (1 Thess 2:4-6)

Once we are freed from these things that chain us, our self-will (flesh) and the self-will of others (people pleasing), we are ready to follow Christ, to flow in his Spirit, to move in his power. The way over is self-surrender and renouncing the need for others to approve of you and your ministry. After all, there is only one Person we have to look in the eye on that final day, and it is his voice we want to hear saying, "Well done, good and faithful servant. Enter into the joy of your Master!"

A *Follower's Prayer*

My Lord God, I have no idea where I am going. I do not see the road ahead of me. I cannot know for certain where it will end. Nor do I really know myself, and the fact that I think that I am following your will does not mean that I am actually doing so. But I believe that the desire to please you does in fact please you. And I hope I have the desire in all that I am doing. I hope from that desire, and I know that if I do this you will lead me by the right road though I may know nothing about it. Therefore I will trust you always though I may seem to be lost and in the shadow of death. I will not fear for you are ever with me, and you will never leave me to face my perils alone. Amen.

— Thomas Merton

Questions for Reflection and Discussion

1. Many pastors and Christian leaders who operate out of "the flesh" have no idea that they are. How can you tell?

2. Learning to discern the guidance of the Spirit is a process. We learn to walk before we run. Usually God instructs us to do one thing, and we get no further instruction until we have been faithful and obedient over that one thing. What does God want you to do? What is the last

thing you remember God instructing you to do? You may have been listening to a sermon, reading your Bible or praying. You may get no further direction until you have done what were you asked to do.

3. What areas of your life are out of alignment with God's revealed will in Scripture? Lack of submission in the obvious things usually equates to a lack of guidance in your life and ministry. Repentance is often the starting place for moving over from life "in the flesh" to life "in the Spirit." Some checkpoints:

- Have you been talking about someone else in a way you wouldn't talk to them (gossip)?

- Do you use the Internet to lust after someone?

- Is there someone you avoid because you haven't forgiven them?

- Do you lack integrity in your financial or business dealings?

- Have you lied or deceived to avoid conflict?

- Do you have a servant spirit about your work or ministry, or are there tasks that you complain about?

- Do you give a generous portion of your income to God's work in the world?

- Are you known for helping the needy and reaching out to the lost and hurting?

- Are you impatient, rude or harsh with people close to you? How about with clerks at the grocery store or maids in a hotel?

4. Relational accountability to people who love and support you is crucial to life lived in the Spirit. How is accountability a guard against abuses of those who have claimed to be led by the Spirit but who have used

such a claim to gain control, get their way or increase their wealth?

5. Which areas of your life are you reluctant to submit to God? Would you be willing to have your calendar and your checkbook broadcast on video for everyone else to see? What would you be ashamed of others knowing about your use of time or money?

6. Who are some people in your life and ministry whom you may have been bowing to in order to avoid conflict or displeasing them? You may have unwittingly given in to designs and directions that are not God's. Seek the Lord in prayer and seek out some wise counselors to find ways to deal with this situation in a gracious way.

7. Fear of loss of control is an issue in everyone's life, whether we are aware of it or not. Giving up control to God is nothing to fear—the fruits are remarkable. Read Psalm 23 and meditate on the blessings and peace we can have when we follow our gentle Shepherd fully.

8. This chapter closes with a prayer by contemplative Thomas Merton. Which parts of that prayer speak to you most? Why?

3

Pay the Price,
Carry the Cross

Indeed, all who want to live
a godly life in Christ Jesus will be persecuted.

2 TIMOTHY 3:12

A life without sacrifice is abomination.

ANNIE DILLARD

Once there was a disciple of a Greek philosopher who was
commanded by his Master for three years to give money
to everyone who insulted him. When this period of trial was over, the
Master said to him: "Now you can go to Athens and learn wisdom."
When the disciple was entering Athens he met a certain wise man
who sat at the gate insulting everybody who came and went.
He also insulted the disciple who immediately burst out laughing.
"Why do you laugh when I insult you?" said the wise man.
"Because," said the disciple, "for three years I have been paying
for this kind of thing and now you give it to me for nothing."
"Enter the city," said the wise man, "it is all yours."
Abbot John used to tell the above story, saying: "This is the door
of God by which our fathers rejoicing in many tribulations
enter into the City of Heaven."

THOMAS MERTON, *THE WISDOM OF THE DESERT*

PAUL HEARD FROM GOD, and followed on the path the Spirit laid out for him. To do this, he denied his own desires and imagination (his "flesh"), and he blocked out the clamoring voices pressuring him to please people. He sensed God's burden continually and lived to please his Master. His leadership bore the fruit. He was a life-giving leader.

Immediately, however, we must come to grips with another indispensable part of Paul's leadership: he paid the price to do what God wanted done. He heard what God wanted him to do, and he unflinchingly pursued God's direction no matter how much it hurt, no matter how great the opposition, no matter what the cost. To understand life-giving leadership, we must understand the essential place that suffering has in the life of a Spirit-led leader. This is a matter of indisputable fact: following Christ will lead to and through painful struggles and horrible opposition. This is an aspect of leadership that we rarely hear discussed but one that we cannot avoid if we want our leadership to be scriptural and our ministry to be life giving. Spiritual leaders center their message on the cross of Jesus and experience the cross of the One they proclaim.

Lemmings and Salmon

Lemmings and salmon are a study in contrasts. Something clicks in the Norwegian lemming population about every four years, and the whole colony of gerbils migrates in search of food while others remain. They migrate across lakes and rivers, cross mountain ranges and eat all the vegetation in their path. Eventually some reach the sea. Attempting to swim it as if it were a lake or a river, they are drowned.

The lemming motto could be, "How could it be wrong if everybody is doing it?" Yet there they go, plunging cultlike to their death. They are a go-with-the-crowd kind of creature, reminiscent of so much accommodation to the culture that many leaders and much of the church have made in our society. Some lemminglike leaders are convinced that suffering is unattractive and unnecessary. They seem unaware that they cannot hear the Lord because their hearing is deafened by listening to the loud voices of culture around them.

In stark contrast is the annual, heroic trek of the salmon. These magnificent fish will swim out of the ocean, upstream, for a hundred miles to fulfill their programming lodged deep in their DNA. At Nimbus Dam in the autumn, near where I grew up in northern California, you can see hundreds of these courageous creatures battle the current and batter their bodies to get up the gates to where they will lay their eggs and die. The cost of the journey does not deter them. The fact that the current is heading strongly in the other direction means nothing to them. They go in the direction they were designed to go, against the current, regardless of the price they must pay.

Lemmings and salmon are wonderful metaphors for two types of leaders. The drummer they hear is different, but they each march to the drumbeat they hear. Lemming-leaders triangulate off the world around them and fulfill the wise truth of the proverb, "There is a way that seems right to a person, but it leads to destruction." Salmon-leaders are models of faithful Christian leadership for the church and for the King of kings. As Jesus put it,

If any want to become my followers, let them deny themselves and take up their cross and follow me. For those who want to save their life will lose it, and those who lose their life for my sake, and for the sake of the gospel, will save it. For what will it profit them to gain the whole world and forfeit their life? Indeed, what can they give in return for their life? Those who are ashamed of me and of my words in this adulterous and

sinful generation, of them the Son of Man will also be ashamed when
he comes in the glory of his Father with the holy angels. (Mk 8:34-38;
Mt 6:24; Lk 9:23)

If we are surrendered leaders, submitted to and following the Lord
Jesus, then we will pay the price. It must feel like we are swimming upstream, and it will seem like most everyone else is going the opposite direction. Like Jesus, all who follow in his steps must be willing to pay the
price of obedience. Any dead fish can float downstream. No lemming
seizes our attention for running with the crowd.

Paul Paid the Price

Paul paid the price. To faithfully follow Jesus is to pay the price, to struggle, to suffer, to encounter opposition to the direction we are going.
This was not any easier to grasp then than it is now.

Timothy wasn't getting it. He had been Paul's closest disciple and
friend, yet he was overwhelmed when Paul was imprisoned near the
end of his life. If we look to Paul's second letter to Timothy, we can read
between the lines that this young disciple was struggling with all that
had happened to Paul. Paul was isolated in jail, bearing all the social
shame and stigma that it meant (2 Tim 1:8). He had been betrayed and
abandoned by everybody in that region (2 Tim 1:15). He does not mention here what kind of physical afflictions he encountered, but he again
and again says he is suffering (2 Tim 1:8, 12; 2:3, 9; 3:11; 4:5). We can only
imagine that he had been physically abused and was struggling with
desperate thoughts in the dark moments and the constant gnawing of
the loneliness worm eating at his emotions.

To all this, Paul invites Timothy to jump in, "Join with me in suffering for the gospel!" (2 Tim 1:8). "What persecutions I endured! Yet the
Lord rescued me from all of them. Indeed, all who want to live a godly

life in Christ Jesus will be persecuted" (2 Tim 3:11-12). These succinct words have a matter-of-fact tone. In fact, Paul's candor is jolting. "All" means everyone and extends to you and me. We cannot wriggle out of this inclusive description of what it means to follow after Jesus. Nor can we weasel out by explaining away what our persecution will look like. "Persecuted" is a rangy word that includes experiencing all kinds of opposition, abuse, antagonism, pressure and pain. To follow Jesus is to swim against the tide of the broken world. Paul's words to Timothy merely reflect Jesus' candid warning that everyone who wants to follow in his footsteps to the kingdom of God must carry the cross of suffering like he did. Everyone.

Why Is It So Hard to Serve Jesus Sometimes?

My wife and I supervised a new church planting team in England several years ago. The team was young, the leader was inexperienced, and the situation was as grim and as challenging as any group of missionaries could want to face. This was a former coal mining area where unemployment was always over 50 percent, and generations of alcoholism and abuse were common. The British would call these people "rough," but in America it would be similar to circumstances in the inner city. "Difficult" and "demanding" are not strong enough words to describe this situation.

There came a time, several months into the church plant, when the honeymoon of good feelings and naïve idealism had worn off, and the team was experiencing significant tension to the point of division. In that low and dark moment, my wife and I were called to avert the crisis that was brewing. I will never forget what one of the team asked me that day: "If Jesus wants his people to serve him, why does he make it so hard?"

Why is it so hard to serve Jesus sometimes? It would have done no good to try to rationalize the question away by suggesting that humans were causing the suffering. My young coworkers would not have bought this. The suffering and struggle were coming directly from their obedience to God. Every step of obedience they took seemed to be accompanied by opposition and struggle. It was hard to do what God wanted done. Did this mean that there was something wrong with what they were doing?

For those who lead and reason "in the flesh," suffering is a sign that something is wrong, that someone is failing, that we should go a different direction. Like Job's friends, carnal leaders interpret struggle as a sign that there is something wrong with the ministry. For those who learn to lead in the Spirit, we come to recognize that suffering and struggle are often signs that we are on the right road, that we are heading the right direction, that we are kicking a dent in the darkness.[1] As Ernst Käsemann says, "Hostility to the cross is the leading characteristic of the world."[2]

Ministry in the Spirit Means Suffering

Pain is a part of God's plan for life-giving leaders and for all who follow Jesus. I must say I am surprised when I hear our contemporaries deny this point. They revert to a "that was then, but not for now" escape clause. On one recent occasion I was speaking on the content of this chapter, and a Christian leader at the back of the room sarcastically chastised me: "Yeah, that will make people want to come and follow Jesus!" As if I had made it up! As if Jesus had not said about the drawing power of the suffering of the cross, "'And I, when I am lifted up from the earth, will draw all people to myself.' He said this to indicate the kind of death he was to die" (Jn 12:32-33). As if Jesus hadn't said that opposition is how we will know you are on the right road (this is what "blessed" means):

Blessed are those who are persecuted for righteousness' sake, for theirs is the kingdom of heaven.

Blessed are you when people revile you and persecute you and utter all kinds of evil against you falsely on my account. Rejoice and be glad, for your reward is great in heaven, for in the same way they persecuted the prophets who were before you. (Mt 5:10-12)

Western Christians have tended to adopt a version of Christianity that cuts out the cross. The civic meeting reported in the newspaper article below could just as easily have been a Christian leaders' meeting like contemporary seminars that advocate removing the cross from our churches, since it is off-putting to so many people:

Religious Symbol Stirs Dispute

Oakland-County officials are asking an artist hired to create a mosaic of local history to redraw a rendering of Mission San Jose so that it doesn't have a cross on its roof. It might offend people, they say.

Supervisors said the cross makes the Fremont mission look more like a church than a mission with historic significance.

Supervisors said they liked county Clerk-Recorder Patrick O'Connell's idea of replacing the cross with a bell on the roof, which might more clearly connote a historic mission.

But the action wasn't welcome news to mission administrator Dolores Ferenz, who said a cross was placed on the mission's roof when built in 1809. "No mission I know of has a bell on the roof," she said.[3]

Might the same thing be said of many churches and Christian leaders today? They have replaced the cross with a Pied Piper's bell, calling people to come without the power of the cross drawing them. No crucified life, no cruciform existence, no life-giving ministry.

No, our struggle and suffering do not show that there is something wrong with us. Like the death of Jesus, our suffering validates that there is something terribly wrong with this world. When we struggle, we join God in what he is doing to redeem this broken world. On the other hand, as Eugene Peterson has said,

> When we avoid this death talk we dishonor the death of Jesus. When we structure our lives to avoid pain and suffering we reject the way of the cross and dishonor the Son. . . . It is common and easy to dishonor the Son by marginalizing His sacrifice. Old timers called this "gnosticism." We can just call it unfaithful. . . . We cultivate the honoring of Jesus the Son by following Jesus to the cross. Sacrifice. Suffering. These are what it means. It is not pragmatic or practical, but what Jesus calls us to.[4]

Paul's Pain, God's Plan

One of the keys to Paul's effectiveness as a life-giving leader is the tremendous price he paid in personal pain, opposition and abuse. I get the impression that many Christian leaders think this was peripheral to Paul's effectiveness, coincidental but not essential. But that is not how Paul sees it. For Paul, the crucified One we preach is congruent with the cruciform life we live:

> For I think that God has exhibited us apostles as last of all, as though sentenced to death, because we have become a spectacle to the world, to angels and to mortals. We are fools for the sake of Christ, but you are wise in Christ. We are weak, but you are strong. You are held in honor, but we in disrepute. To the present hour we are hungry and thirsty, we are poorly clothed and beaten and homeless, and we grow weary from the work of our own hands. When reviled, we bless; when persecuted, we endure; when slandered, we speak kindly. We have be-

come like the rubbish of the world, the dregs of all things, to this very day. (1 Cor 4:9-13)

Notice that Paul does not place the blame for his suffering on "this terrible world" or "this evil Roman Empire" or "petty and jealous people." Instead, he identifies God's design as the source of suffering. "I think God has exhibited us apostles as last of all, as though sentenced to death."

In 2 Corinthians, Paul uses a technical term to describe the integral relationship of his suffering with his ministry. In 2 Corinthians 2:14, he writes, "But thanks be to God, who in Christ always leads us in triumphal procession, and through us spreads in every place the fragrance that comes from knowing him."

This translation of the NRSV and almost every English translation glosses over Paul's use of the participial form of *thriambeuō*. The English translation above could give the impression that all is sweetness and light in Christ, because we participate in the celebration of his triumphal procession. But this is a misunderstanding. In fact, Paul implies again here what he says explicitly in 1 Corinthians 4.

A *thriambolos* was a very specific type of slave. Normally, these were high-status people, usually kings and rulers, who had been captured in war and were paraded to show Rome's power and invincibility, demonstrating the negative outcome for any who stand against Caesar.[5] Paul adapts the metaphor and applies it to himself as a slave of Christ, bound and dragged at the end of Christ's glory parade throughout the empire to show the glory of Christ. As Victor Paul Furnish translates this verse more accurately, "To God be thanks, who in Christ always puts us on display (as if we were prisoners in a triumphal procession), and who manifests through us the fragrance of the knowledge of him in every place."[6] The New Living Translation is one of the few contemporary English versions to capture this sense: "But thanks be to God, who made us his captives and leads us along in Christ's triumphal procession. Now wherever we go he uses us to tell others about the Lord and to spread the Good News like a sweet perfume."

This makes much better sense of the verses that follow. Onlookers have two quite different responses to Paul and his ministry, depending on where they are with Christ. For those who are in Christ, who have "eyes to see and ears to hear," Paul's death march is a tribute to the crucified and resurrected Jesus. For those walking in the flesh, Paul's struggles confirm their bias: he is no servant of God. For them, Paul and his ministry are merely the "smell of death."

Our Suffering Reveals the Savior: The Cruciform Life

To come to Christ is to come to the crucified and risen One. The life-giving apostle embodies in himself the crucifixion of Jesus in the sufferings and struggles he endures as he is faithful and obedient to his Lord. So Paul preaches the crucified and risen Jesus, and he embodies the dying of Jesus in his struggles to further point to the Savior. His message is about the cross and his life is cruciform, shaped to look like the cross. In a telling passage he says,

> But we have this treasure in clay jars, so that it may be made clear that this extraordinary power belongs to God and does not come from us. We are afflicted in every way, but not crushed; perplexed, but not driven to despair; persecuted, but not forsaken; struck down, but not destroyed; always carrying in the body the death of Jesus, so that the life of Jesus may also be made visible in our bodies. For while we live, we are always being given up to death for Jesus' sake, so that the life of Jesus may be made visible in our mortal flesh. (2 Cor 4:7-11)

This is surely what Paul is getting at in Galatians when he says, "I have been crucified with Christ; and it is no longer I who live but Christ who lives in me" (Gal 2:19-20). As Charles Cousar puts it,

> Paul's ministry is an example of what living under the shadow of the cross entails. He mentions afflictions, perplexities, persecutions, and the like not as a special badge he wears as an apostle, but as evidence of what the church continually discovers when taking seriously the crucified Jesus. Religion in general may be tolerated or even revered by a surrounding society, but the cross will evoke rejection.[7]

Many leaders have not come to grips with this crucial role suffering and opposition play in the lives of life-giving leaders. When we engage a truly broken world, we pay the price of embracing the brokenness. Suffering is a barometer of faithfulness and an essential method for communicating our message about the crucified and risen One. In our suffering we embody his grace and Spirit: "Always carrying in the body the death of Jesus, so that the life of Jesus may also be made visible in our bodies" (2 Cor 4:10). Failure to suffer is a failure to model the life-giving death of Jesus.

This is no minor theme in Paul's letters. We can sample statements from his other letters that point to the same necessity of suffering for those who are faithful to the gospel:

> *But my friends, why am I still being persecuted if I am still preaching circumcision? In that case the offense of the cross has been removed. (Gal 5:11)*

> *The only reason they do this is to avoid being persecuted for the cross of Christ. (Gal 6:12 NIV)*

> *I pray therefore that you may not lose heart over my sufferings for you; they are your glory. (Eph 3:13)*

> *I want to know Christ and the power of his resurrection and the sharing of his sufferings by becoming like him in his death, if somehow I may*

attain the resurrection from the dead. (Phil 3:10-11)

I am now rejoicing in my sufferings for your sake, and in my flesh I am completing what is lacking in Christ's afflictions for the sake of his body, that is, the church. (Col 1:24)

And you became imitators of us and of the Lord, for in spite of persecution you received the word with joy inspired by the Holy Spirit, so that you became an example to all the believers in Macedonia and in Achaia. (1 Thess 1:6-7)

This is evidence of the righteous judgment of God, and is intended to make you worthy of the kingdom of God, for which you are also suffering. (2 Thess 1:5)

Do not be ashamed, then, of the testimony about our Lord or of me his prisoner, but join with me in suffering for the gospel, relying on the power of God. . . . For this gospel I was appointed a herald and an apostle and a teacher, and for this reason I suffer as I do. But I am not ashamed, for I know the one in whom I have put my trust, and I am sure that he is able to guard until that day what I have entrusted to him. (2 Tim 1:8, 11-12)

Now you have observed my teaching, my conduct, my aim in life, my faith, my patience, my love, my steadfastness, my persecutions and suffering the things that happened to me in Antioch, Iconium, and Lystra. What persecutions I endured! Yet the Lord rescued me from all of them. Indeed, all who want to live a godly life in Christ Jesus will be persecuted. (2 Tim 3:10-12)

Already in this chapter I have cited from every letter of Paul except 1 Timothy, Titus and Philemon. Each citation above has profound and binding things to say about the expectation we should have to suffer if we are ministering in the Spirit. It may seem tedious, but I list citations from across the Pauline corpus of letters to underscore three crucial points:

1. Suffering is a major, not a minor, theme in Paul's understanding of Spirit-led ministry and leadership.

2. Suffering was a shared experience of early Christians.

3. Suffering is a standard for how to know we are on the right road as Christians. As Paul bluntly says, "All who want to live a godly life in Christ Jesus will be persecuted" (2 Tim 3:12). Jesus says it in different words: "Blessed are you when people revile you and persecute you and utter all kinds of evil against you falsely on my account. Rejoice and be glad, for your reward is great in heaven, for in the same way they persecuted the prophets who were before you" (Mt 5:11-12). "Blessed" means, "This is how you know you are on the right road."

Paul's Corrective in 2 Corinthians

If all that is not enough, we must come to grips with Paul's teaching in 2 Corinthians 10—13 that faithful leaders who suffer are a corrective to false leaders and therefore false conceptions of the Christian life.

Someone had come among the Corinthians raising doubts that Christ was speaking through Paul (2 Cor 13:3). It is not too difficult to uncover what their reasons were. Paul even is aware of their arguments: "For they say, 'His letters are weighty and strong, but his bodily presence is weak, and his speech contemptible'" (2 Cor 10:10; cf. 11:6). They claimed they were "superior" apostles (2 Cor 11:5) because of their Jewish pedigree (2 Cor 11:22), their superior speaking ability (highly valued in Corinthian culture) and their wonder-working ability (2 Cor 12:12).

The issue is not simply that they have different styles of leadership, theirs polished and Paul's uncouth. Paul claims that their approach to ministry is a reproach because they, by their words and example, have been preaching "another Jesus," not the one who was crucified for our sins: "For if someone comes and proclaims another Jesus than the one we proclaimed, or if you receive a different spirit from the one you received, or a different gospel from the one you accepted, you submit to it readily enough" (2 Cor 11:4).

Earlier, before Jesus was crucified, this was the same problem Peter was having when he first heard Jesus describe the way of the cross as his way to save the world. Peter surely conceived, like many of his contemporaries, that the Messiah was to be a victor who would wrest power from Rome and re-establish the glory days of David's kingdom. Peter cannot even hear it when Jesus says that he must go to the cross, suffer and die. So convinced was Peter that he had it right that he took Jesus "aside and began to rebuke him" (Mk 8:32). Jesus calls this impulse satanic and tells Peter he is reasoning according to human wisdom and not according to God's divine plan.

Paul encounters the same kind of response to his suffering apostleship in Corinth. His counter is to claim that faithful leaders suffer like Jesus did. Rather than having it all together, faithful leaders have learned that true power and true ministry flow from a complete awareness of God's power rather than the leader's perfection or polish. Therefore he claims, "If I must boast, I will boast of the things that show my weakness" (2 Cor 11:30). And, "Therefore, to keep me from being too elated, a thorn was given me in the flesh, a messenger of Satan to torment me, to keep me from being too elated. Three times I appealed to the Lord about this, that it would leave me, but he said to me, 'My grace is sufficient for you, for power is made perfect in weakness.' So, I will boast all the more gladly of my weaknesses, so that the power of Christ may dwell in me. Therefore I am content with weaknesses, insults, hardships, persecutions, and calamities for the sake of Christ; for whenever I am weak, then I am strong" (2 Cor 12:7-10).

For Paul, this conception of leadership is not a theological option but a God-given imperative. To lead according to human wisdom and utilizing human power and strategies is to lead toward "another Jesus." To lead and live a cruciform life, a life conformed to the cross and sufferings of Jesus, is to reveal in our lives and teaching the crucified One. When Jesus died on the cross he undid the way of power and human machinations, "disarming the rulers and authorities and made a public example of them, triumphing over them in it [the cross]" (Col 2:15). The way of Jesus is the way of leadership from a place of weakness and dependence on God's power and authority (see Mt 20:20-27).

I.C.F.D.

Since suffering is a necessary, normal and expected part of faithful Christian leadership, a quality leaders need most is I.C.F.D. This stands for Incredible Capacity for Disappointment.

Pain and opposition are extremely discouraging. That is why Paul must say, "So let us not grow weary in doing what is right, for we will reap at harvest time, if we do not give up" (Gal 6:9).

In a revealing, emotional passage Paul underscores the human difficulty of bearing the weight of leadership in Christ's kingdom: "We are afflicted in every way, but not crushed; perplexed, but not driven to despair; persecuted, but not forsaken; struck down, but not destroyed" (2 Cor 4:8-9). Our troubles are temporary in comparison with the eternal kingdom that is coming: "So we do not lose heart. Even though our outer nature is wasting away, our inner nature is being renewed day by day. For this slight momentary affliction is preparing us for an eternal weight of glory beyond all measure" (2 Cor 4:16-17).

It is revealing to list what Paul considered "this slight momentary affliction" in 2 Corinthians 6; 11: great endurance, afflictions, hardships, calamities, beatings, imprisonments, riots, labors, sleepless nights, hunger, dishonor, ill repute, treated as impostors, punished and yet not killed, sorrowful, poor, having nothing, countless floggings, often near death, "five times I have received from the Jews the forty lashes minus one" (2 Cor 11:24), "three times I was beaten with rods," (2 Cor 11:25), "once I received a stoning" (2 Cor 11:25), "three times I was shipwrecked" (2 Cor 11:25), "for a night and a day I was adrift at sea" (2 Cor 11:25), on frequent journeys, in danger from rivers, in danger from bandits, in danger from his people, in danger from Gentiles, in danger in the city, in danger in the wilderness, in danger at sea, in danger from false brothers and sisters, in toil and hardship, through many a sleepless night, hungry and thirsty, often without food, cold and naked, "and, besides other things, I am under daily pressure because of my anxiety for all the churches" (2 Cor 11:28).[8]

These are Paul's "slight momentary afflictions!" They are physical, emotional, social, mental and psychological. They cannot be limited to merely physical pain or social opposition. Suffering is suffering. And yet he can conclude later when writing to the Christians in Rome: "I consider that the sufferings of this present time are not worth comparing with the glory about to be revealed to us. . . . Who will separate us from the love of Christ? Will hardship, or distress, or persecution, or famine, or nakedness, or peril, or sword? As it is written, 'For your sake we are being killed all day long; we are accounted as sheep to be slaughtered.' No, in all these things we are more than conquerors through him who loved us" (Rom 8:18, 35-37). He knew exactly what he was talking about.

A parable is told of a farmer who owned an old mule. The mule fell into the farmer's well. The farmer heard the mule braying—or whatever mules do when they fall into wells. After carefully assessing the situation, the farmer sympathized with the mule but decided that neither the mule nor the well was worth the trouble of saving. Instead, he called his neighbors together, told them what had happened and enlisted them to help haul dirt to bury the old mule in the well and put him out of his misery.

Initially the old mule was hysterical. But as the farmer and his neighbors continued shoveling and the dirt hit the mule's back a thought struck him. It suddenly dawned on the mule that every time a shovel load of dirt landed on his back he should shake it off and step up. This he did, blow after blow. "Shake it off and step up . . . shake it off and step up . . . shake it off and step up," he repeated to encourage himself. No matter how painful the blows or distressing the situation seemed, the old mule fought panic and kept right on shaking it off and stepping up.

It wasn't long before the old mule, battered and exhausted, stepped triumphantly over the wall of the well. What seemed as if it would bury him blessed him, all because of the manner in which he handled his adversity. The afflictions that come along to bury us usually have within them the potential to benefit and bless us and bless others.[9]

"This slight momentary affliction is preparing us for an eternal weight of glory beyond all measure" (2 Cor 4:17). If we are faithful, we are living for one reward on that day when we stand together with all the martyrs and leaders who have gone before us. We will be gathered before all the royalty, all the nobles, all the prophets and priests, in front of Abraham, Moses, David, in the presence of the disciples and martyrs and forebears in the faith, at the foot of Jesus with God's radiance shining all around. We live for that day when God will say so everyone can hear: "Well done, good and faithful servant. Enter into the joy of your master." If we maintain an incredible capacity for disappointment, we will reap an indescribable reward.

Questions for Reflection and Discussion

1. Read 1 Peter 4:12-14 and Mark 13:5-27 (parallels in Mt 24; Lk 21). Reflect and discuss.

2. Not all suffering is a sign of faithful leadership. If we suffer for doing wrong, that is a different matter. Sometimes we struggle when we do something we are no good at. There is the persistent presence of the problem of evil, that is, suffering that makes no sense and has no explanation whatsoever. Also, bull-headed, arrogant leaders asserting their power in the flesh may very well suffer because they do not listen and trust others around them. Discuss.

3. What are the costs for you if you really go for it? What opposition do you anticipate?

4. Do your preaching and teaching contain the "offense of the cross," or has pressure caused you to filter out the difficult claims of the gospel? Read 1 Corinthians 1—2 and discuss.

5. Have you fully weighed what leading for Jesus will cost you? Do you understand that following Jesus means seeking the way of serving and obscurity? Read Matthew 20:20-27 and discuss.

4

GOD'S POWER IN
CRACKED POTS

*But we have this treasure in clay jars, so that it may be made clear that
this extraordinary power belongs to God and does not come from us.*

2 CORINTHIANS 4:7

*It is our weakness, not our competence, that moves others;
ours sorrows, not our blessings, that break down the barriers of fear and
shame that keep us apart; our admitted failures, not our paraded
successes, that bind us together in hope.*

LARRY CRABB

*The desire we so often hear expressed today for "episcopal figures,"
"priestly men," "authoritative personalities" springs frequently enough
from a spiritually sick need for the admiration of men, for the
establishment of visible human authority, because the genuine authority
of service appears to be so unimpressive. There is nothing that so
sharply contradicts such a desire as the New Testament itself in its
description of a bishop (1 Tim. 3:1ff.). One finds there nothing
whatsoever with respect to worldly charm and the brilliant
attributes of a spiritual personality. The bishop is the simple,
faithful man, sound in faith and life, who rightly discharges his*

duties to the Church. His authority lies in the exercise of his ministry.
In the man himself there is nothing to admire.

DIETRICH BONHOEFFER

A WATER BEARER IN INDIA HAD TWO LARGE POTS, each hung on opposite ends of a pole that he carried across his neck. One of the pots had a crack in it, while the other pot was perfect and always delivered a full portion of water at the end of the long walk from the stream to the master's house. The cracked pot arrived only half full.

For a full two years this went on daily, with the bearer delivering only one and a half pots full of water to his master's house. Of course, the perfect pot was proud of its accomplishments by comparison, perfect to the end for which it was made. But the poor cracked pot was ashamed of its imperfection and miserable that it was able to accomplish only half of what it had been made to do.

After two years of what it perceived to be a bitter failure, it spoke to the water bearer one day by the stream. "I am ashamed of myself, and I want to apologize to you." "Why?" asked the bearer. "What are you ashamed of?" "I have been able, for these past two years, to deliver only half my load because this crack in my side causes water to leak out all the way back to your master's house. Because of my flaws, you have to do all of this work, and you don't get full value from your efforts," the pot said.

The water bearer felt sorry for the old cracked pot, and in his compassion he said, "As we return to the master's house, I want you to notice the beautiful flowers along the path." As they went up the hill, the old cracked pot took notice of the sun warming the beautiful wildflowers on the side of the path, and this cheered it some. But at the end of the trail, it still felt bad because it had leaked out half its load, and so again the pot apologized to the bearer for its failure.

The bearer said to the pot, "Did you notice that there were flowers only on your side of the path, but not on the other pot's side? That's because I have always known about your flaw, and I took advantage of it. I planted flower seeds on your side of the path, and every day while we walk back from the stream, you've watered them. For two years I have been able to pick these beautiful flowers to decorate my master's table. Without you being just the way you are, he would not have this beauty to grace his house."

All Clay Pots Are Cracked Pots

This parable pictures very clearly the biblical imagery of 2 Corinthians 4:7. There Paul asserts that we are fragile pots, common and vulnerable, mere vessels for God's purpose, power and glory: "But we have this treasure in clay jars, so that it may be made clear that this extraordinary power belongs to God and does not come from us."

Paul makes it explicit that this is God's intentional strategy to reveal his glory. God is intensely interested in us not confusing where the power comes from and where the glory is due. That is why there is the purpose statement, "so that." God puts the treasure of the "light of the knowledge of the glory of God in the face of Christ" (2 Cor 4:6) in common, fragile vessels so that "it may be made clear that this extraordinary power belongs to God and does not come from us" (2 Cor 4:7).

By the end of 2 Corinthians, Paul virtually expands the metaphor from us being clay pots to cracked pots. Jesus said to him, "My grace is sufficient for you, for power is made perfect in weakness" (2 Cor 12:9). Paul draws the inference: "So, I will boast all the more gladly of my weaknesses, so that the power of Christ may dwell in me." With these words, Paul launches a cultural earthquake. He claims that God's glory leaks out through the cracks in our pots and is not seen in our shine, gloss and polish.

Greeks idolized cultured speech and powerful bodies and perfected form. They looked down their noses at things weak, frail and flawed. They valued "self-sufficiency" (*autarkeia*), the ability to rise above all temporal circumstances. To them Paul says God's way is to use the things that are "weak" to reveal his grace and his glory. The word he uses for "weak" (*astheneia*) is an opposite of "self-sufficient." The word he uses for "weak" has quite a range and includes weakness, sickness, illness, flaws and powerlessness. Paul applies the message of the gospel to his leadership style and declares that the way God works through leaders is done in such a manner as to communicate the in-breaking of his kingdom in a world that has idolized the creation and its creatures.

This is what is so wrong, even dangerous, about the recent trend of Christian leaders adopting the "commitment to excellence" fad in the business world. I'm not saying we should have a commitment to schlock, but our excellence is not that which "makes clear" that the power comes from God and not from us. When a commitment to excellence means that ordinary folk are no longer viewed as able to do ministry (as I have seen this trend work itself out), we have become more Corinthian and less Christian in our leadership.

We are all too interested in power, then and now. To the mother of two of his disciples, Jesus explicitly says that her and their desire for power and prestige is not Jesus' way. Instead, those who are followers of Jesus do not "lord" it over others but seek to serve and become "slaves of all" (Mt 20:20-27). The problem remains with us. A recent bestseller that shows this dark interest humans have in power is *The 48 Laws of Power*. Among the forty-eight laws are "Get others to do the work for you, but always take the credit," "Learn to keep people dependent on you," "Use selective honesty and generosity to disarm your victim," and "Keep others in suspended terror: cultivate an air of unpredictability."[1]

God's strategy is to work out the scandal of the cross in the lives of Christians. To a world focused on power, prestige and pride, Jesus' crowning achievement is to go low to the shame of the cross. This is how spiritual warfare is accomplished, to come in an opposite spirit. So too, the Spirit works out the gospel in the body of Christ by choosing lowly, "weak" people—cracked pots—to reveal God's redemption of the least, the last and the lost. Our weakness is an intentional contrast to a world self-absorbed with power, strength and image. Christians may thumb their noses at Friedrich Nietzsche's philosophy of *der Übermensch* ("superman"), the ideal of a powerful, independent soul who needs no one else, even God. But a casual observer may more easily compare much of what masquerades for Christianity with Nietzsche's power ideal than with Jesus' focus on vulnerability and service and Paul's conviction that God's power most often shows through our weakness.

God's way is to choose the unlikely and undeserving to expose those who think they are more deserving and worthy of recognition and salvation. In a telling passage in 1 Corinthians, Paul writes:

For the message about the cross is foolishness to those who are perishing, but to us who are being saved it is the power of God. For it is written, "I will destroy the wisdom of the wise, and the discernment of the discerning I will thwart." Where is the one who is wise? Where is the scribe? Where is the debater of this age? Has not God made foolish the wisdom of the world? For since, in the wisdom of God, the world did not know God through wisdom, God decided, through the foolishness of our proclamation, to save those who believe. For Jews demand signs and Greeks desire wisdom, but we proclaim Christ crucified, a stumbling block to Jews and foolishness to Gentiles, but to those who are the called, both Jews and Greeks, Christ the power of God and the wisdom of God. For God's foolishness is wiser than human wisdom, and God's weakness is stronger than human strength. Consider your own call, brothers and sisters: not many of you were wise by human standards, not many were powerful, not many were of noble birth. But God chose what is foolish in the world to shame the wise; God chose what is weak in the world to shame the strong; God chose what is low and despised in the world, things that are not, to reduce to nothing things that are, so that no one might boast in the presence of God. He is the source of your life in Christ Jesus, who became for us wisdom from God, and righteousness and sanctification and redemption, in order that, as it is written, "Let the one who boasts, boast in the Lord." (1 Cor 1:18-31)

God maintains the "divine incognito" of Jesus' ministry in ours by pouring out his power on the unlikely and the imperfect. Those who look for God at the top of the heap do not see God down at the feet going low. Those expecting Messiah to turn up at a meeting of the temple power brokers are surprised when he is found in the manger by shepherds and astronomer/astrologers. He visits the temple later on, but he hangs out at the Samaritan's well and the house of a tax collector, and he is accompanied and anointed by sinful people. To ensure that no one is confused, God associates his kingdom with the weak of the world. He wants no one to mistake his glory for the world's power.

Cathy's Story

A few years ago, this principle was put to the test for me. I was approached by Cathy[2] and asked if she could come on one of our Share Jesus! teams. She had been diagnosed with bipolar disorder and strug-

gled with the emotional swings from high to low. There were two reasons Cathy approached me. One was that she had made progress
through counseling, drug therapy and group work and felt like she had
come to a good place and was ready to "get back into the game" as a
Christian servant. The other reason she approached me was because of
a sermon I preached on this subject. She had come from a perfectionistic church background in which everyone kept their problems hidden
and "faked good" to present themselves as nice Christians. She was
wounded in that environment when she reached out to her pastor from
a psychiatric unit and was given the impression that "real" Christians
aren't manic-depressive.

An evangelistic mission team is a high-stress environment, and I was
concerned that the pressure of the work might adversely affect Cathy.
As a brother in Christ, though, I was more concerned that I would practice something other than I preached and stick my finger in an old
wound that left her feeling sub-Christian and subhuman. We made ar-
rangements for my wife to be on the same team so she could watch over
Cathy and take the initiative if she had a manic or depressive episode. I
never understood Paul's teaching in the Corinthian correspondence
like I did this week watching God use Cathy.

The third morning of the mission, it was Cathy's turn to give her testimony at a gathering of the church people before they initiated their
outreach to the nearby junior high school that day. Cathy was nervous
on the old adage, "Once burned, twice shy." She had been rejected
from a church before because she had shared her struggles, but she decided that this time she would be honest and tell how God had helped
her through her struggle, how grace had ministered to her wounds, and
how she like Paul had prayed for this thorn to be removed without avail.
Though she still struggled she wanted to witness to God's grace and
goodness amid the battle.

A group of women showed up who had been meeting together for several years. None of them had admitted and so none of them realized that several people in the room had struggled with a bipolar disorder or had husbands, siblings or children who struggled with this problem. They had been meeting together for prayer and encouragement for a long time but had "faked good" and suffered silently, never sharing the deepest burden they were carrying.

When Cathy shared her testimony, God's power turned that superficial fellowship into a time of deep sharing and caring. Tears flowed freely, and many felt the relief of coming out of the shadows and being known and accepted by their fellow Christians. Cathy too, it seemed, was delivered from the deep soul wound of rejection by sharing openly that she was weak, and yet God's grace was present. By the end of the week she had led three junior high girls to make a commitment to Christ and to become a part of that church. Never again would she wonder if God could use someone broken like her. She embodied what Paul wrote to the Corinthians: "But God chose what is foolish in the world to shame the wise; God chose what is weak in the world to shame the strong; God chose what is low and despised in the world, things that are not, to reduce to nothing things that are, so that no one might boast in the presence of God" (1 Cor 1:27-29).

Unfortunately, so many churches and Christian leaders today are afraid of people who appear weak. They maintain a myth of perfectionism and "fake good" for one another, never seeing how their pretension destroys the grace and life that could come through the body of Christ if they were only real and humble with each other. Churches like this tend to have four unbreakable commands that are never spoken but widely understood by all those who participate:

Rule 1: Don't have anything wrong with you.

Rule 2: If you do, get over it quickly.

Rule 3: If you can't get over it quickly, then fake it.

Rule 4: If you can't get over it quickly or fake it, then stay away from me. I don't want anyone to think I have it too.

These are the same four rules that drive alcoholics and are the unspoken law of many a dysfunctional family. Some summarize this as the "no talk" rule—don't tell anyone your problems.

Cathy had languished in just such a church. There were no bootstraps she could pull herself up by, and even if she could grab them she didn't have the strength within herself to stop being bipolar. The unspoken Four Laws of Perfectionistic Churches came through to her, and she got the message loud and clear: you are not welcome here.

We live in a country that is rapidly secularizing in every way. When those outside the church accuse Christians of being hypocrites, this is exactly what they are referring to. They see Christians as having all the same foibles, problems and struggles that they have with the difference that they perceive Christians to pretend they do not have such problems. To them, we are naked emperors, strutting about in our invisible and unreal suits of superiority and togetherness. In reality, we are just as exposed as everyone else. We all have obvious problems that we can't get over quickly or fake. Into just such people God chooses to pour his glory and his grace.

If we think about it for a moment, the kind of person who is drawn to church because "everyone there seems to have it together" still has to go through another conversion to the crucified One who calls us to take up our cross and follow him. Someone pursuing perfection might just as well be drawn to Mormonism as to Christianity, and Mormons have perfected the image of polish and every hair in place. This is not reality. Utah has the highest rate of spousal abuse, and Baptists and Methodists, traditional teetotalers by denomination, have the highest rates of alcoholism (Jews and Catholics are among the lowest). Even the myth of small-town morality compared with urban decay has recently crumbled with the revelation that studies show that teenage drug use and alcohol abuse are significantly higher in small towns than in urban areas.[3] Whether we admit it or not, we are all sinners in deep need of grace and help. God's only choice for Christian leaders is the weak who must rely on his strength to do what he asks.

Recently Governor Jesse Ventura of Minnesota and media mogul Ted Turner came out with their versions of Karl Marx's "Christianity is an opiate for the masses." One, a former Navy Seal and professional wrestler turned politician, and the other an independent and wealthy entrepreneur, jabbed, "Jesus is a crutch for the weak." Said Ventura, "Organized religion is a sham and crutch for weak-minded people who need strength in numbers."[4] What are we tempted to answer in reply? If our tendency is to deny this, then we are tempted to sell out the real gospel. We should not be embarrassed by such criticisms. Instead, if we are honest with ourselves and biblical in our theology, we should proudly claim, "Jesus is much more than a crutch. He is a whole hospital! Where would I be without Jesus?" Effective outreach to unchurched people today is emergency-room ministry. If they allow us into their world to help them, we find them bruised, battered and broken. Jesus cries out now as back then, "How I would gather you under my wings like a mother hen her chicks." How Jesus would have compassion on them because they are needy sheep without a shepherd!

The Corinthian concern with image, power and perfection tore at the fabric of the body of Christ and threatened the authenticity of the gospel in that place. First, there was a bunch of people who believed themselves to be second-class citizens, or no citizens at all. They were made to feel that because they did not have certain gifts, they were not a part of Christ's body. No doubt, the way they were rudely treated at the Lord's Supper (1 Cor 11) undergirded their conviction that they didn't matter to God. To these weak people Paul says,

> If the foot would say, "Because I am not a hand, I do not belong to the body," that would not make it any less a part of the body. And if the ear would say, "Because I am not an eye, I do not belong to the body," that would not make it any less a part of the body. If the whole body were an eye, where would the hearing be? If the whole body were hearing, where would the sense of smell be? But as it is, God arranged the members in the body, each one of them, as he chose. (1 Cor 12:15-18)

In the same way Paul has to chastise the strong. Because of God's preference to pour his glory and wisdom into the weak and foolish vessel, there are no second-class citizens. In God's economy, those who judge another's importance by how they appear, how wealthy they are or by how much ability they have are judging wrongly, "in the flesh."[5] In the Spirit, God has valued each person equally and often surprises us by whom he chooses to use most:

> The eye cannot say to the hand, "I have no need of you," nor again the head to the feet, "I have no need of you." On the contrary, the members of the body that seem to be weaker are indispensable, and those members of the body that we think less honorable we clothe with greater honor, and our less respectable members are treated with greater respect; whereas our more respectable members do not need this. But God has so arranged the body, giving the greater honor to the inferior member, that there may be no dissension within the body, but the members may have the same care for one another. If one member suffers, all suffer together with it; if one member is honored, all rejoice together with it. Now you are the body of Christ and individually members of it. (1 Cor 12:21-27)

What Cracks in Our Pots Communicate

In the Thorton Wilder play *The Angel That Troubled the Waters*, a doctor comes to the healing pool to be cured of his melancholy. The play is based on the tradition about the pool in Bethesda (Jn 5): when the angel stirs up the water the first one in receives healing from his or her ailment. When the angel sees the doctor he denies him the chance to get in the water:

> Doctor, without your wounds, where would your power be? It's your melancholy that makes your low voice tremble into the hearts of men and women. The very angels themselves cannot persuade the wretched on this earth as can one human being broken on the wheels of living. In love's service, only wounded soldiers can serve.

We are all wounded warriors. We all find God working graciously and amazingly through our wounds and weakness. "In love's service, only wounded soldiers can serve." Paul models this in his first letter to Timothy: "The saying is sure and worthy of full acceptance, that Christ Jesus came into the world to save sinners—of whom I am the foremost. But for that very reason I received mercy, so that in me, as the foremost, Jesus Christ might display the utmost patience, making me an example to those who would come to believe in him for eternal life" (1 Tim 1:15-16).

Paul, "the chief of sinners," was chosen by Christ so that he could demonstrate his "utmost patience," his kindness and his mercy. Paul, a former murderer and persecutor of the church, is an "example" to everyone else. If Jesus can forgive and use Paul, then he can forgive and use anybody for his glory and his purpose.

On that score, the recent Promise Keepers movement is doing the very thing that needs to be done in our land. The heart of PK, as it is called, is a call to men to recognize their weakness and brokenness and to help one another through support and accountability groups to walk faithfully and humbly amid their temptations. Even the organization of Promise Keepers is modeling this dependence in a powerful way as it goes through a time of downsizing and reorganizing to focus on its mission rather than maintaining a large institutional edifice.

This is why Jesus so highly values children and says any who want to enter the kingdom of God must do it like a little child. A child, like a clay jar, is a symbol of weakness, vulnerability and frailty. To such as these, says Jesus, belong the kingdom of God. Jesus is pleased to use frail children, single mothers, those with physical deformities and psychological disorders, people with problems and needs and hurts, those who struggle with anger, fear, pride and lust—people like me and you. He pours out his power on cracked pots to show where the power comes from and to whom the glory is due.

Questions for Reflection and Discussion

1. Are you a part of a fellowship, prayer group, Bible study, home group, Sunday school class or cell group where you can honestly share your life and your struggles and receive support and be held accountable? If not, what steps can you take to structure such a group?

2. What are the cracks in your pot, your weaknesses, through which God makes his grace evident to others? Usually we have to rely on others to give us this feedback.

3. Reflect on and discuss the story about Cathy. In what ways does your church include or exclude people with problems from doing ministry?

4. Who might be left out of doing ministry in your church? Teens? Single adults? People with handicapping conditions? Someone else?

5. What do you think of Thorton Wilder's statement, "In love's service, only wounded soldiers can serve"?

6. Reflect on and discuss: "Jesus is not simply a crutch; he's a whole hospital."

7. Discuss the Four Laws of Perfectionistic Churches. To what extent are these true or untrue for your church?

5

THE POWER OF
PERSONAL EXAMPLE

Show yourself in all respects a model of good works.

TITUS 2:7

*Remember your leaders, those who spoke the word of God to you;
consider the outcome of their way of life, and imitate their faith.*

HEBREWS 13:7

You can teach people what you know, but you reproduce who you are.

ZIG ZIGLAR

From one example, learn about everything.

VIRGIL

IN THE EARLY CHURCH THERE WAS A TENDENCY among some to
focus on Jesus' spiritual nature so much that they virtually denied that he
had a physical nature or even a human experience. They conceived of
Jesus as some sort of spiritual apparition appearing in human form but
not taking on material substance. The early church leaders spotted the
danger of this right away. If Jesus wasn't really human, then he really didn't

suffer on the cross for our sins and we are still under judgment. These gnostics, so called because of their emphasis on knowledge of special truths (*gnōsis* is the Greek word for knowledge), were resoundingly rejected. To some who had gnostic tendencies, 1 John makes a strong emphasis on confessing the humanity of Christ: "Beloved, do not believe every spirit, but test the spirits to see whether they are from God; . . . for by this you know the Spirit of God: every spirit that confesses that Jesus Christ has come in the flesh is from God" (1 John 4:1-2). Their problem was not with Jesus' divine nature but that he became a real human being. "Fully God, fully human"—that is our confession about Jesus.

There was a practical, ethical outworking of this heresy in the early church, as evident in another major theme of 1 John. People who think that physical experience does not matter tend to make their relationship with God a purely spiritual relationship that has no apparent effect on their relationships with others in the church. To them, John writes that it is not possible to love God and hate a brother or sister in the Lord. The command to love God is intricately enmeshed with the command to love one another. By cultivating a relationship with other Christians, we grow our relationship with God, and vice versa. By his incarnation, by his teaching and by his example Jesus demonstrated that spiritual salvation works itself in relational reconciliation with others (see, for example, Mt 18). Matter matters to God; people matter more. The early church was wise to wholly reject gnosticism and its teachers.

Throughout the history of the church, the gnostic heresy has mutated and reappeared in various forms. Recently it has manifested itself in gnostic conceptions of leadership, best characterized by a bumper sticker that I purchased a few years ago: "Don't follow me. Follow Christ!"

Perhaps on first reading this bumper sticker has some appeal. It puts

Christ at the center, and it displays a sense of humility and one's rightful place next to Christ. But, as we shall see below, this is the opposite of what Paul teaches about the power of personal example.

In fact, this do-as-I-say-not-as-I-do principle does not work, and no one follows it, except for perhaps Christian leaders attempting to shirk their crucial role of modeling. It not only matters what preachers say. Who they are and how they live is all-important for their credibility and the fruit that their ministry produces. For example, one can preach about generosity all day, but no one listens if the leader does not live this out. If the treasurer knows the leader skimps in financial contributions, and the personnel committee observes a leader who is tight with others' salaries but then contends for his or her own, and the finance committee observes someone who is fearful and controlling, then what was preached about money becomes meaningless. The leader's practice speaks so loudly that others can hardly hear what is said.

Imagine trying to raise children on the do-as-I-say-not-as-I-do principle. You can coach about etiquette all you want, but if you talk with food in your mouth, so will your children. Our actions speak so loudly others cannot hear what we are saying when there is a discrepancy. Gnostic leadership does not work for raising children, and it does not work in the church. As Zig Ziglar has said, "You can teach people what you know, but you reproduce who you are." The principle of leadership by example cannot be violated. We always model something, either positive or negative.

The Imitation of Paul

I was surprised to learn that I had imbibed a gnostic conception of leadership very early in my Christian life. When I was in seminary in the early 1980s, I was looking for a book in the New Testament section of the library to complete a paper I had been assigned. When I found my book, I was shocked by one next to it titled *The Imitation of Paul*.[1] My first response, in good seminarian fashion, was to grab the book so I could punch holes in its sub-Christian argument. Everyone knows the center of the Christian life is the adoration and imitation of Jesus, not Paul, I thought to myself.

I was stopped in my tracks when I opened up to the table of contents. I was stunned. This book was an exegetical study of the eleven times Paul says, "Be imitators of me" and similar things: 1 Corinthians 4:14-17; 11:1; Galatians 4:12; Ephesians 4:32; Philippians 3:17; 4:9; 1 Thessalonians 1:6-7; 2:14; 2 Thessalonians 3:7-9; 1 Timothy 4:12; Titus 2:7-8. I had unconsciously bought the "don't follow me, follow Christ" mentality. This providential circumstance began a decade-long journey that culminated in my doctoral dissertation, now published as *Paul's Paradigmatic "I": Personal Example as Literary Strategy*.[2] In that study, I go beyond the explicit texts that call his readers to imitation, to a letter-by-letter study of how Paul continually grounds his ethical and theological argument in his practice and example. The most celebrated examples are Romans 7, 1 Corinthians 9, and Galatians 1—2, but the technique is evenly spread throughout Paul's letters to those who knew him personally. He boldly links his teaching and precept to his example and model. If he wasn't practicing what he preached, then it seems unlikely that his letters would have been collected and canonized. There has long been recognized a literary distinction between *show* and *tell*. As Wayne Booth puts it, everything an author "shows" serves also to "tell," and "the line between showing and telling is always to some degree an arbitrary one."[3] Powerful written communication does both, and so does effective leadership.

Paul again and again makes it clear that this is his conscious and deliberate leadership approach. Near the beginning of his first letter to the Corinthians, Paul reminds them that he was their spiritual parent, and they therefore should "imitate" his example.

> *For though you might have ten thousand guardians in Christ, you do not have many fathers. Indeed, in Christ Jesus I became your father through the gospel. I appeal to you, then, be imitators of me. For this reason I sent you Timothy, who is my beloved and faithful child in the Lord, to remind you of my ways in Christ Jesus, as I teach them everywhere in every church. (1 Cor 4:15-17)*

If you read this from a gnostic leadership mode, you may experience revulsion at Timothy's marching orders. Timothy is to remind them of Paul's ways in Christ, "as I teach them everywhere in every church." We might have expected Paul to say, "Read the Bible; learn about Jesus' ways." There are two reasons he could not and would not say this. First, the New Testament had not yet been collected in one place, and it may well be that all four Gospels achieved their final form well after 1 Corinthians was penned. Second, at least 95 percent of the people throughout the Roman Empire were illiterate. The apostles and their leaders were the only gospel most of them would ever read.

Instead, Timothy is sent to help them remember the visual, living model of life "in Christ" that Paul had embodied. This is a powerful coaching tool. First, Paul has modeled behavior that they are to imitate. Second, they are "reminded," that is, remembering rather than learning afresh what it means to live under the kingdom of God. Third, because Paul and Timothy can live this way, so too are they encouraged that they are able to walk this way "in Christ," in the power of the Spirit God has granted them when they transferred from the kingdom of darkness to the kingdom of his blessed Son.

In the chapters that follow, Paul presents his personal example several times as a part of the argument and exhortation: what to do with a man involved in an illicit affair (1 Cor 5:3); what to do with sexual immorality in the church (1 Cor 6:12); marriage (1 Cor 7:7); and what to do about the troublesome issue of idol meat (1 Cor 8:13—9:27). After introducing his personal example in 1 Corinthians 4 and laying it out in the exhortation of 1 Corinthians 5—10, Paul summarizes again this crucial leadership technique: "Be imitators of me, just as I also belong to Christ. I commend you because you remember me in everything and maintain the traditions just as I handed them on to you" (1 Cor 11:1-2).

I have used my translation above because the NIV is misleading with "Follow my example as I follow the example of Christ." The words "follow the example" do not appear in Paul's Greek. "Of Christ" (*Christou*) is a possessive genitive, which I have translated as "I belong to Christ." Support for this is drawn from Paul's technical and polemical usage of the possessive form "of Christ" as an identifier that one is a Christian.[4] In other words, "of Christ" is part of Paul's shorthand for "Christian." The most obvious example of this for an English reader is in 1 Corinthians 1:12, where Paul has to correct the divisive identity some were claiming as "I am of Paul, I am of Apollos, I am of Peter." What Paul wants them to know is that they are one body because they all are "of Christ." That is, they belong to Christ. In the same way, by 1 Corinthians 11, the term "of Christ" echoes with the same connotation. Paul is their example for emulation because he is "of Christ," as they are.

Another way to look at this is "of Christ" in 1 Corinthians 11:1 is synonymous for "in Christ" in 1 Corinthians 4:17. To be "in Christ" is to be in the new sphere operating under Christ's control, in accordance with Christ's impulses and mind. Paul is confident that the Corinthians are able to emulate him because they too are "in Christ." Paul merely models what is possible for all those who have entered the sphere of Christ's power and control. His example shows them the Christian life is possible, practical and attainable. The model Paul has set announces, "Here's how."

We see this same principle operating in other letters of Paul:

Brothers and sisters, join in imitating me, and observe those who live according to the example you have in us. (Phil 3:17)

Keep on doing the things that you have learned and received and heard and seen in me, and the God of peace will be with you. (Phil 4:9)

And you became imitators of us and of the Lord, for in spite of persecution you received the word with joy inspired by the Holy Spirit, so that you became an example to all the believers in Macedonia and in Achaia. (1 Thess 1:6-7)

We also constantly give thanks to God for this, that when you received the word of God that you heard from us, you accepted it not as a human word but as what it really is, God's word, which is also at work in you believers. For you, brothers and sisters, became imitators of the churches of God in Christ Jesus that are in Judea, for you suffered the same things from your own compatriots as they did from the Jews. (1 Thess 2:13-14)

Now we command you, beloved, in the name of our Lord Jesus Christ, to keep away from believers who are living in idleness and not according to the tradition that they received from us. For you yourselves know how you ought to imitate us; we were not idle when we were with you, and we did not eat anyone's bread without paying for it; but with toil and labor we worked night and day, so that we might not burden any of you. This was not because we do not have that right, but in order to give you an example to imitate. (2 Thess 3:6-9)

Let no one despise your youth, but set the believers an example in speech and conduct, in love, in faith, in purity. Until I arrive, give attention to the public reading of scripture, to exhorting, to teaching. Do not neglect the gift that is in you, which was given to you through prophecy with the laying on of hands by the council of elders. Put these things into practice, devote yourself to them, so that all may see your progress. Pay close attention to yourself and to your teaching; continue in these things, for in doing this you will save both yourself and your hearers. (1 Tim 4:12-16)

Show yourself in all respects a model of good works, and in your teaching show integrity, gravity, and sound speech that cannot be censured; then any opponent will be put to shame, having nothing evil to say of us. (Tit 2:7-8)

The DNA Principle: Doing Flows Out of Being

Unlike technique driven leadership teaching, Paul's practice is character-based. His life-giving leadership flows out of the life God has imparted to him "in Christ." Leadership is not so much about task effectiveness, management ability, vision casting or time efficiency. Leadership is about modeling life in Christ.

J. Robert Clinton has studied character-based leadership at length in *The Making of a Leader: Recognizing the Lessons and Stages of Leadership Development.*[5] He studies this principle in the lives of biblical and historical figures and emphasizes the indisputable pattern he has recognized: God does something in his leaders before he does something through them. God is about the business of making us more and more like Jesus. As our core character is changed more and more into the likeness of Christ, we become more effective and more fruitful in our leadership. Leadership development, then, is not about what we do or how we do it but about who we are from the inside out. Doing flows out of being. Effective leadership flows out of transformed character.

We can call this the DNA principle of leadership development. The old adage is true: Christianity is not so much taught as caught. People see in us Christ and his kingdom—or not. Christianity is not simply cognitive (a set of beliefs) or behavioral (a set of actions), but it is emotional and spiritual and social, involving all we are and all our relationships. That is why Jesus called his disciples to be with him. They would learn as much in what they observed and overheard as in what they recorded of his formal sayings. The spiritual dynamics of submission to Christ, trust and obedience in his lordship, transforming grace and merciful compassion, deep trust in prayer and radical obedience in all our affairs, and so forth, can only be absorbed as we are around others who are "in Christ." Right statements cannot possibly convey the whole of the Christian life. Only fathers or mothers "in Christ" can flesh out for us life in the Spirit. Christian leaders are meant to be "Jesus with skin on."

Another way to say this is busyness does not build the kingdom of God. God's Spirit erects the kingdom of God. We more and more cooperate with the movement of God's Spirit as we become more and more like Christ, in our core being, in our thoughts, in our feelings and in our behaviors. Conversion is more than behavioral, so leadership needs to be as well. The kingdom of God grows as more and more people become more and more submitted to and flowing in God's will and purpose.

The practical implication of this point is that life-giving leaders must focus on who they are in Christ. Prayer is not an optional extra, nor is personal Bible reading. Gifted speakers may be able to deliver energetic messages for years without transforming the lives of those who hear, if they are not living out life "in Christ." Life-giving leadership flows out of life in Christ, walking with God humbly day in and day out. Since the effectiveness of what we do flows out of the character of who we are, being and becoming are the focus. Committees, groups and tasks in a life-giving church need to pay attention to the DNA. What matters is not what we are doing and how much we are accomplishing but the kingdom character with which we conduct our business and how we treat people in the process.

The Power of Negative Examples

There are three cultural observations we can make about our society that accentuate the need for leaders to model life in Christ. First, Gen Xers and the emerging generations tend to focus on transparent relationships and genuine spirituality and show little tolerance for loyalty to people or organizations that do not seem real or authentic. Second, in the video orientation of our society, a picture paints a thousand words. If a picture paints a thousand words, a video paints a million words, and a Christian's life is a whole library about what it means to live and move "in Christ." Third, due to some highly publicized moral scandals of some Christian leaders and because of a widespread experience of inauthentic Christians, there is high resistance to hypocrisy. People of all ages are looking for examples who are real and authentic—the genuine article.

The point is, we cannot *not* model as leaders. We always model something, positive or negative. If we decide to neglect Paul's example of the power of personal example, we still must deal with the fallout of a life lived differently than the message we proclaim. A low-commitment herald tends to produce a spectator audience that listens to the gospel, puts money in the plate and samples the programs offered by the church (this has become normal in North American Christianity). A high-commitment leader preaches and lives fanatical dedication to Christ and reproduces radical disciples who live to make a difference in the world for Christ.

Dallas Willard makes the point that we should explain to people the cost of non-discipleship: bondage to sin, missing the liberty God offers in Christ, bearing the weight of guilt, missing out on the eternal experience of life in Christ. In the same way we should consider the cost of nonmodeling as leaders: disconnect of followers, low commitment, distrust, shallowness in relationships, inauthenticity and lack of life-giving power in the ministry. There is a tremendous cost to nonmodeling, just as there is an attendant power in personal example. As the old adage goes, "Your walk talks and your talk walks. But your walk talks further than your talk walks."

Questions for Further Reflection and Discussion

1. Discuss the theology of "Don't follow me. Follow Christ!"

2. What part does modeling play in your leadership and teaching?

3. If your way of life is "the only gospel some people may ever read," what are they reading about God and his kingdom by how they see you live?

4. What aspects of your core being need transformation for you to be more effective as a leader? What characteristics of your church?

5. What role do grace and God's Spirit play when we fail to model Christ for others?

6

THE POWER OF
PARTNERS

I planted, Apollos watered, but God gave the growth.
So neither the one who plants nor the one who waters is anything,
but only God who gives the growth. The one who plants
and the one who waters have a common purpose,
and each will receive wages according to the labor of each. For we are
God's servants, working together; you are God's field, God's building.

1 CORINTHIANS 3:6-9

Much Christian leadership is exercised by people who do not know
how to develop healthy, intimate relationships and have opted for
power and control instead. Many Christian empire builders
have been people unable to give and receive love.

HENRI NOUWEN

It is obvious that teams outperform individuals.

JON R. KATZENBACH AND DOUGLAS K. SMITH

SYNERGISM IS THE PRINCIPLE THAT two or more people working together in the same direction can accomplish more than the sum of them working individually. A famous illustration of this is the study done on two horses. The first one could pull ten thousand pounds on a sled behind. The second could pull fourteen thousand pounds. What would you think they could pull harnessed together in the same direction? Most people would guess something like twenty-four thousand pounds, but the answer is forty-nine thousand pounds! The sum is greater than a combination of the parts. Of course, there is a negative implication too. If the horses were allowed to pull in different directions, the total amount they could pull is far less than what they could pull individually.

It works this way in ministry too. When we work together in the same direction, the sum of our efforts is far greater than what we could accomplish individually. Paul uses *synergos*, the Greek word "synergism" comes from, to describe his coworkers as those who "work with" him in the gospel labor. He also calls them partners (*koinōnos*; *koinōnia*). For Paul, ministry in the Spirit is ministry in partnership among coworkers. In a Lone Ranger world, we are rightly reminded by Paul that powerful ministry—synergism in the Spirit—happens when we share the ministry, build teams and rely on one another in the power of the Spirit.

We have enough cowboy Christian leaders. The Marlboro Man image of the independent and self-sufficient man is almost a cliché for the kind of leadership we reject in the church. And yet, so many people conceive of their leadership in exclusively individual terms like, "I am the leader; you are the followers." "I am the pastor here, and these are *my* people" (which has a larger theological problem with it!). "My vision is what matters because I am *the* leader." "We're not doing what some of the people in the church want because it doesn't fit with *my* vision." The Marlboro Man is alive and well.

Paul's Theology of "We" and the Heresy of "Me"

To the extent that these caricatures are true of leadership in the church, the heresy of "me" has polluted our life-giving ability. The leadership of rugged individualism reflects the brokenness of the world, not the redemption plan that God has revealed in Jesus and commanded us to work out through the community of the church. The CEO conception of leadership, which may be an indispensable component of large-program congregations in the United States, is hardly God's new plan for leadership. In a world context, the CEO leader who has immense control and authority looks more like the "lord it over" leadership that Jesus condemns in Matthew 20 than it does the self-lowering leadership that Jesus models in Philippians 2.[1]

Our conception of leadership in the body of Christ must be a theology of "we." It is a team effort. Even secular writers point out the challenge for businesses in the individualistic West to build high-performing teams. And they candidly say individualism is the reason teams do not happen: there is a "natural resistance to moving beyond individual roles and accountability."[2] In scriptural terms we would label that resistance "the flesh." Alienation, isolation and an "all by myself" arrogance are the bitter fruits of the fall of Adam and Eve and the fallen nature that each of us inherits.

By contrast, when we come "into Christ"—a favorite and important theological expression in Paul, parallel to the crucial "in Christ"—two things happen at the same time: we are reconciled to God, and we become a part of a new community that is reversing the effects of the Fall. We begin to get reconnected. We start to become interdependent. We find ourselves experiencing a deeper sense of God's grace and presence as we are enfolded into the body of people who are "in Christ." Christianity is a team sport. Lone Ranger Christians are either ex-Christians or are unhealthy spiritually, failing to have the indispensable element of fellowship as a part of their spiritual diet. The principle "outside the church there is no salvation" (*extra ecclesium nulla salus*) is a scriptural principle, when we understand "church" in the broad sense of being a part of a local body rather in the narrow sense of belonging to a particular denominational brand of Christianity.

To be a Christian leader—to lead "in Christ," in Paul's terms—is a team effort in which each person contributes gifts and the whole is much healthier and stronger than any individual. A clear example of this issue is seen in Paul's first letter to the Corinthians. He dismisses their divisiveness over individual leaders as evidence that they were not walking by the life-giving leadership of the Holy Spirit but were walking in the death-giving life "in the flesh." By prizing individualistic leadership over the united ministry of Christ's one body they were making a mockery of the redemption, reconciliation and reconnecting work Christ has done by drawing us into the one body. To them Paul writes,

> *For it has been reported to me by Chloe's people that there are quarrels among you, my brothers and sisters. What I mean is that each of you says, "I belong to Paul," or "I belong to Apollos," or "I belong to Cephas," or "I belong to Christ." Has Christ been divided? Was Paul crucified for you? Or were you baptized in the name of Paul? (1 Cor 1:11-13)*

Paul spends the first three chapters of his letter confronting this attitude. We need to let the magnitude of this observation set in. He treats unity first and foremost before he addresses such issues as a man sleeping with his stepmother (1 Cor 5), lawsuits and sexual immorality (1 Cor 6), idol meat (1 Cor 8—10), abuses in worship (1 Cor 11—14) and a highly deficient understanding of the resurrection of Jesus (1 Cor 15). We can infer that the issue of individualism and factionalism is a more pressing problem. After all, no one will ever hear about the resurrection power of Jesus if the body of Christ blows apart. Given the importance of these other issues, this should tell us how important the "we" and not merely the "me" of life "in Christ" is for Paul and should be for us.

Paul directly attacks an individualistic practice of leadership:

> For when one says, "I belong to Paul," and another, "I belong to Apollos," are you not merely human? What then is Apollos? What is Paul? Servants through whom you came to believe, as the Lord assigned to each. I planted, Apollos watered, but God gave the growth. So neither the one who plants nor the one who waters is anything, but only God who gives the growth. The one who plants and the one who waters have a common purpose, and each will receive wages according to the labor of each. For we are God's servants, working together; you are God's field, God's building. (1 Cor 3:4-9)

The whole emphasis is on God's initiative and activity in the body of believers. Does a leader make a church? No, God does because "only God . . . gives the growth" (1 Cor 3:7). Paul says that those with leadership gifts are a part of God's team, by God's choice, through the ability God manifests through them. Neither Paul nor Apollos "is anything" (1 Cor 3:7) without God's working through them. Instead, leaders serve a "common purpose"—God's purpose, not their agendas. The reason is we are God's coworkers (*synergoi*).[3] We join God in what he is doing in his "field," his "building." (This is what is so off base about a pastor who makes a possessive claim of "my people!") And so Paul can summarize his correction: "So let no one boast about human leaders. For all things are yours, whether Paul or Apollos or Cephas or the world or life or death or the present or the future—all belong to you, and you belong to Christ, and Christ belongs to God" (1 Cor 3:21-23).

The first three chapters of 1 Corinthians contain Paul's direct corrective to individualistic conceptions of ministry and leadership. In 1 Corinthians 12 Paul spells out his positive vision of what it means to be "in Christ," to experience Christ's life-giving presence through the community of believers. Because to be "in Christ" is inseparable from being in the community and fellowship with Christ's people, he exhorts the Corinthians to understand the unity and interdependence that have come from their entering life in the Spirit through faith in Jesus Christ.

Since there are "varieties" of gifts, services and tasks to be performed by God's people, it is possible for rugged individualists to think their thing is the most important thing and their gifting is the most important spot on the team. Paul reiterates what he said in the earlier chapters: there is only one Spirit, the same God who is working through each and every gift and ability (1 Cor 12:4-6). The individuals' gifts are given to them to exercise on behalf of "the common good." The emphasis remains on the unity that we have because of the one God who is exercising these gifts (1 Cor 12:8-11). Because God is the unifying factor of the body, division and individualism are clear indicators that one is not God's coworker.

Paul paints the picture in as many ways as he possibly can.

For just as the body is one and has many members, and all the members of the body, though many, are one body, so it is with Christ. For in the one Spirit we were all baptized into one body—Jews or Greeks, slaves or free—and we were all made to drink of one Spirit. Indeed, the body does not consist of one member but of many. (1 Cor 12:12-14)

Consequently, Paul points out that the playing field is leveled for us all. Those who think their ministry does not matter because they do not have another's gifts or because they do not think that what they are doing is important are mistaken (1 Cor 12:15-31). The role each of us plays in the body is according to God's assignment by God's will (1 Cor 12:18). Whether we think it is important or not does not matter. It is God's work, so whatever assignment we have been given is a divine appointment and therefore has essential significance. Logically it follows that none of us can look down at other parts of the body by thinking we do not need them or that they are unessential and expendable (1 Cor 12:21-31). The church is a boat we are on together. It is ultimate foolishness to think we can sink their part of the ship without getting wet ourselves. The love chapter that follows (1 Cor 13) is not about marriage, though we often hear it read at weddings, but in context is applied to the relational essentials for life "in Christ" with other Christians.

Paul's "theology of we," as I have called it, calls us to act and lead in new ways as a part of the redeemed. The "heresy of me" directly contradicts the reconciling work God is up to. The Fall breaks us apart. Redemption brings us back together. Individualistic leaders model brokenness, not redemption. Only team leadership can portray the correct picture of new life in Christ and in Christ's body.[4]

Paul's Partnership Language

Paul practices what he preaches. Paul's "theology of we" works itself out in an understanding of membership in the church as sharing partner responsibilities. *Koinonia* became a word popularized in the 1970s to describe the relational side of being a Christian. It is a direct transliteration of the Greek word *koinōnia*. This word and its related *koinōnos* are variously translated in the NRSV as "partnership," "fellowship," "sharing," "participation" or "communion." It is clear for Paul that *koinōnia* is much more than spilling coffee on one another after church. Paul uses *koinōnia* in three ways that together portray his understanding that to come into Christ is to come into a real partnership relationship with others who are in Christ.

First, *koinōnia* has the meaning of committed, sharing relationships. To come into Christ is to experience a real bond with the Lord *and* with the Lord's people. To become a Christian is to be restored into a relationship with Jesus and to be called into the community of the redeemed: "God is faithful; by him you were called into the fellowship of his Son, Jesus Christ our Lord" (1 Cor 1:9). To experience the grace and love of God is to become united with God in the family of his people: "The grace of the Lord Jesus Christ, the love of God, and the *communion* (*koinōnia*) of the Holy Spirit be with all of you" (2 Cor 13:13). *Koinōnia* is something that comes from God and is birthed by God through the Holy Spirit in the community.

This understanding of the vertical and horizontal dimensions of partnership in Christ are most crisply seen in Paul's words to the Corinthians:

> *The cup of blessing that we bless, is it not a sharing* (koinōnia) *in the blood of Christ? The bread that we break, is it not a sharing in the body of Christ? Because there is one bread, we who are many are one body, for we all partake of the one bread. Consider the people of Israel; are not those who eat the sacrifices partners* (koinōnoi) *in the altar? What do I imply then? That food sacrificed to idols is anything, or that an idol is anything? No, I imply that what pagans sacrifice, they sacrifice to demons and not to God. I do not want you to be partners* (koinōnous) *with demons. You cannot drink the cup of the Lord and the cup of demons. You cannot partake of the table of the Lord and the table of demons.* (1 Cor 10:16-21)

It is clear that this is an exclusive partnership bond. Our relationship with Jesus and his people is not one partnership among many but one that is analogous to marriage fidelity (see Eph 5:21-33).

Because we are partnered with Jesus and other Christians in the community of the redeemed, Paul can write in his second letter to the Corinthians, "Do not be mismatched with unbelievers. For what partnership (*metochē*) is there between righteousness and lawlessness? Or what fellowship (*koinōnia*) is there between light and darkness?" (2 Cor 6:14). "Fellowship" is definitely too weak a translation of *koinōnia* here. Paul is not saying Christians should have no social relationships with non-Christians but that we should not be bound in loyalties like marriage with them.

The second way Paul uses *koinōnia* is to refer to the financial implications that a shared partnership entails. This use of the Greek word parallels the Latin *societas*, "partnership," a legal relationship among equals according to Roman law.[5] Because the churches are partners in his missionary endeavor, they support him by their prayers, by sending helpers and by providing financial support for the ongoing missionary work. "Those who are taught the word must share (*koinōneitō*) in all good things with their teacher" (Gal 6:6).

The Philippians are perhaps Paul's most significant partners in his work. The tone of his letter to them is the most personal and warm among all of his letters. He begins by expressing how grateful he is for their partnership, "because of your sharing in the gospel from the first day until now" (Phil 1:5). Their concrete expression has been to send a helper in Epaphroditus (Phil 2:25), who risked "his life to make up for those services" the Philippians could not provide themselves (Phil 2:30). This concrete help is not merely spiritual but entails their financial commitment to Paul's work:

In any case, it was kind of you to share (synkoinōneō) *my distress. You Philippians indeed know that in the early days of the gospel, when I left Macedonia, no church shared with me in the matter of giving and receiving, except you alone. For even when I was in Thessalonica, you sent me help for my needs more than once. Not that I seek the gift, but*

I seek the profit that accumulates to your account. I have been paid in full and have more than enough; I am fully satisfied, now that I have received from Epaphroditus the gifts you sent, a fragrant offering, a sacrifice acceptable and pleasing to God. (Phil 4:14-18)

Partnership is not a spiritual reality that can be separated from physical and social implications. To share fellowship in the Spirit is to be a part of one body, which is to say when one part has a difficulty or need, then all parts share in it. The Philippians had fully grasped this implication of the gospel in their tangible partnership with Paul in his work. Elsewhere Paul applies this same understanding of fellowship and partnership to the relationship of his churches to the poor among the Christians in Jerusalem and the collection he was gathering for them (Rom 15:26-27; 2 Cor 8:3-5; 9:13).

Paul's third use of *koinōnia* brings the first two together in the sense of a real working partnership between two coworkers or co-owners of an enterprise. This is how he understood his relationship to the apostles in Jerusalem: "and when James and Cephas and John, who were acknowledged pillars, recognized the grace that had been given to me, they gave to Barnabas and me the right hand of fellowship (*koinōnias*), agreeing that we should go to the Gentiles and they to the circumcised" (Gal 2:9).

"Fellowship" here should be understood in the deepest sense of a working partnership. Paul, Barnabas, James, Peter and John come to a working agreement that will guide their future missionary endeavors. Paul and Barnabas are to focus on the Gentile aspect of the mission field, and the pillar apostles are to focus on the Jewish element.

We can see this same understanding of sharing the work together undergirding Paul's relationships with other Christians. Paul writes to Philemon about his slave Onesimus, "So if you consider me your partner, welcome him as you would welcome me" (Philem 17). About Titus he writes, "As for Titus, he is my partner and co-worker in your service; as for our brothers, they are messengers of the churches, the glory of Christ" (2 Cor 8:23).

Paul's partnership theology is also indicated by how he refers to his many coworkers. T. R. Glover was the first person to point out Paul's fondness for words compounded with the prefix *syn*, which means "with" or "co-." These compounds, said Glover, have two main functions: to emphasize Paul's union with the crucified and risen Christ and to emphasize his partnership in working with other Christians to spread the gospel.[6] Paul calls his partners in the missionary work "coworkers," "coprisoners," "coslaves," "cosoldiers" and "colaborers."

- *coworker* (*synergos*, Rom 16:3, 7, 9, 21; 2 Cor 8:23; Phil 2:25; 4:3; Col 4:7, 10, 11, 14; Philem 1, 24)
- *coprisoner* (*synaichmalōtos*, literally "fellow prisoner of war," Col 4:10; Philem 23)
- *coslave* (*syndoulos*, Col 1:7; 4:7)
- *cosoldier* (*systratiōtēs*, Phil 2:25; Philem 2)
- *colaborers* (*synathleō*, Phil 4:2-3)

Paul's Partnership Theology in Action

Paul's partnership theology was not merely a matter of words. We can see it work out in how he conducted the missionary enterprise entrusted to him and his coworkers. To take one example, Paul sends Timothy to handle the Corinthian situation instead of coming himself (1 Cor 4:17). Timothy was entrusted with handling one of the most explosive situations in the New Testament church we have on record. If Paul were operating in an individualistic mode, he would have handled this himself. But instead he sends a true partner in the missionary work to handle the knotty problems of sexual morality, lawsuits, idol meat, disorderly worship and faulty views about the resurrection. To be sure, Paul sends a letter with

Timothy, but Timothy is left to answer questions and see that the situation is handled appropriately. Paul practices what he teaches: mission is partnership (see Phil 2:19-30; 1 Thess 3:2-5).

Another example is the case of how Paul addresses Philemon and his community together in treating the issue of Philemon's slave, Onesimus. In the individualistic culture we live in, we might find it quite alien that Paul writes to Philemon and the whole church meeting at his house regarding the issue of Philemon's personal property, Onesimus (Philem 1-2). Our individualism might lead us to ask, "This has nothing to do with the church. Why does Paul include the church in the conversation?" But our question would be equally bizarre to Paul. To him, of course he would write to the church. We are all part of one body. The things that affect two of us (Philemon and his slave Onesimus) affect us all. All ethics, in Paul's mind, are community ethics. Our life in Christ necessarily entails a community application of our ethics. So Paul approaches it from a "we," not a "me," perspective: "So if you consider me your partner, welcome him as you would welcome me" (Philem 17). Paul writes to Philemon and his church because the whole church is affected by the ethical decisions of its individual members.

Paul's Partners in Ministry

It is worth noticing another piece of evidence of Paul's partnership theology. In Paul's thirteen brief letters, more than one hundred people are identified as his coworkers and partners in ministry.[7] Over and above these we know by name, a host of unnamed friends and coworkers is referred to.[8] Here are some of the key names of his coworkers, whose names may sound familiar to us.

Ananias. Paul's first partner as a Christian. In one fell swoop Paul had lost his standing as a Pharisee when he acknowledged Christ as Lord.

With his reputation as a persecutor, no Christians were going to be eager to come alongside Paul. Ananias, under the insistence of the Holy Spirit, came alongside Paul and gave him the needed assistance while his eyes healed. He may well have been the person who baptized Paul (Acts 9:18).

Barnabas. He provided the needed introductions to the apostles when Paul came to Jerusalem (Acts 9:27). Later he persuaded Paul to assist him in Antioch, and they spent a fruitful year together. They launched out on the first missionary journey together.

Silvanus, called Silas in Acts, was one of the three who brought the gospel to Thessalonica and Corinth, along with Paul and Timothy. He is mentioned as the coauthor of 1 Thessalonians. A cosufferer with Paul at Philippi (1 Thess 2:2; Acts 16:19-24), he was Paul's only missionary partner who was also a Roman citizen (Acts 16:37-38).

Timothy of Lystra, Paul's most prominent coworker, is listed in the superscription in six of Paul's thirteen letters, and two more are addressed to him from Paul. He was a native of Lystra, the son of a Jewish mother and a Greek father, but he was raised by his mother, Eunice, in the Jewish faith. He was probably converted to Christ by Paul's visit to Lystra at the same time as his mother when Paul visited there (Acts 14:6-7), and that is why Paul refers to him as "my true son in the faith" (1 Tim 1:2).

Luke the physician. The author of Acts identifies himself as Paul's traveling companion in the "we" passages (those beginning in Acts 16:10; 20:5; 27:1) where Luke's third-person narrative ("they," "them") gives way to a first-personal record ("we," "us"). Paul refers to him three times in his letters (Col 4:14; 2 Tim 4:11; Philem 24). He traveled with Paul to places like Philippi, Jerusalem and Rome. Obviously he thought well of Paul, since Paul is center stage as the hero of the book of Acts.

Priscilla and Aquila (Rom 16:3; 1 Cor 16:19; 2 Tim 4:19). Priscilla is named first, suggesting a higher-status background for her. She belonged to an ancient and illustrious Roman family. "In secular society of the time, when one finds a wife being named before her husband, the reason usually is that her social status was higher than his."[9] Aquila was a tentmaker (or perhaps *skēnopoios* may have the wider sense of "leather worker"). Luke records:

> *After this Paul left Athens and went to Corinth. There he found a Jew named Aquila, a native of Pontus, who had recently come from Italy with his wife Priscilla, because Claudius had ordered all Jews to leave Rome. Paul went to see them, and, because he was of the same trade, he stayed with them, and they worked together—by trade they were tentmakers. (Acts 18:1-3)*

Paul's connection with them was fortuitous indeed. They probably planted the church in Rome, and later provided introduction for him when he went to the empire's capital. He met them in Corinth, and they served together during some difficult years in Ephesus.

Apollos of Alexandria. Probably he had been a member of the very large Jewish community in Alexandria, since he "was an eloquent man, well-versed in the scriptures" (Acts 18:24). Priscilla and Aquila heard him speak and realized he was a believer in Jesus who needed some of the gaps in his knowledge filled in.

Titus. Probably one of Paul's converts (Tit 1:4), he accompanied Paul and Barnabas to Jerusalem (Gal 2:1), and as a Gentile convert served as the living test case for what they were going to require of Gentile converts. He was the helper Paul sent to Corinth in the midst of some of his fiercest conflicts there to sort things out.

Onesimus of Colossae. This slave came to Paul as an *amicus domini* ("friend of the master" law) and became a Christian in the process. The

brief story is found in the letter to Philemon, the shortest of Paul's letters. Later, in Colossians 4, in a passage where Paul is identifying himself and his coworkers as "slaves of Christ," it is no small thing that he
does not make reference to Onesimus in this manner. Instead, the
former slave has become one of Paul's valued coworkers and is honored
as "the faithful and beloved brother" (Col 4:9).

Many Others

Mark (Col 4:10; Philem 24)

Aristarchus (Col 4:10; Philem 24)

Andronicus and Junia, probably a husband and wife team[10] who
    were "eminent apostles" (Rom 16:7)

Philemon (Philem 1)

Epaphroditus (Phil 2:25), the same as Epaphras (Col 1:7; Philem
    23)

Clement (Phil 4:3)

Urbanus (Rom 16:9)

Jesus Justus (Col 4:11)

Demas (Col 4:14; Philem 24), who later abandoned Paul (2 Tim
    4:10)

Tychicus (Col 4:7); "the rest of my co-workers whose names are in
    the book of life" (Phil 4:3)

Archippus (Philem 2)

Euodia (Phil 4:2-3)

Syntyche (Phil 4:2-3)

Tertius, who took dictation of the letter to the Romans
    (Rom 16:22)

Phoebe (Rom 16:1)

Erastus (Rom 16:23)

Quartus (Rom 16:23)

Tryphaena (Rom 16:12)

Tryphosa (Rom 16:12)

Persis (Rom 16:12)

Mary (Rom 16:6)

Onesiphorus (2 Tim 1:16-18)

Reproduction, Not Production

Many Christian leaders tend to think about leadership in terms of achievement of goals or production of a program that is measured in terms of the number of people who came or the amount of money that was raised and spent. The focus of life-giving leadership is quite different. It is not about production of a product but about reproducing the life of Christ in individuals and the congregation. Reproduction of the life of the Spirit is the focus.

Do you want to multiply your ministry? Do you want to increase, expand and enlarge your impact for the kingdom of God? The focus needs to be on building and birthing partners for the work. Paul succinctly states this operating principle to Timothy: "You then, my child, be strong in the grace that is in Christ Jesus; and what you have heard from me through many witnesses entrust to faithful people who will be able to teach others as well" (2 Tim 2:1-2).

Paul envisions four generations of leadership development in this short exhortation: Paul's leadership, Timothy's leadership, those Timothy equips and those they go on to equip. Reproduction, not production, is the key to effective ministry.

Questions for Reflection and Discussion

1. What best describes your leadership philosophy—CEO leadership or teamwork? How would others describe your style?

2. Read Philemon. How would you have handled the situation with

Onesimus? What is there about Paul's community ethic that excites or bothers you?

3. Who are your key partners in ministry? How have you recognized or affirmed them lately?

4. Who are you discipling and mentoring as a believer? How and in whom are you reproducing yourself?

7

THROUGH PRAYER

*I pray that, according to the riches of his glory, he may grant that you may
be strengthened in your inner being with power through his Spirit.*

EPHESIANS 3:16

*I am grateful to God—whom I worship with a clear conscience,
as my ancestors did—when I remember you constantly
in my prayers night and day.*

2 TIMOTHY 1:3

If God would make you greatly useful, He must teach you how to pray.

CHARLES SPURGEON

*What seems missing in the bewildering maze of programs is an emphasis
on prayer equal to the strong reliance on action—as if strategy,
management and goals are what really count.*

DAVID RAMBO

*The central question is, Are the leaders of the future truly men and
women of God, people with an ardent desire to dwell in God's presence,
to listen to God's voice, to look at God's beauty, to touch God's
incarnate Word and to taste fully God's infinite goodness?*

HENRI NOUWEN

Let us not think that waiting on the Lord will mean getting less done.
Who can do the most, you or the God of heaven and earth? Is not the
central problem of our generation that the world looks upon the church
and sees it trying to do the Lord's work in the flesh?

FRANCIS SCHAEFFER

THE STORY IS TOLD OF A GIFTED CONCERT PIANIST from Eastern Europe who was touring the United States. His performances drew the well-heeled of society to formal affairs in major cities across the country. At one concert, a mother and father took their rambunctious twelve-year-old son. Stiffly dressed in a tuxedo, he clearly felt uncomfortable in this formal environment and was bored waiting while the local aristocracy promenaded to their seats.

While his parents were preoccupied in a conversation with a business associate, the young boy left his seat and began exploring the auditorium. He quickly found his way up onto the stage. Without thinking about what he was doing, he sat down at the ebony grand piano placed center stage, flooded with spotlights. No one seemed to notice him, until he began to play.

With all his heart he pounded out the only song he knew: "Chopsticks." The crowd instantly became silent and turned their collective glare on this insolent boy at the piano. Of course, his parents were stunned when they realized it was their son. What could they do?

Meanwhile, backstage, the concert pianist heard what was going on. He looked through the side curtains of the stage and realized what was happening. Without pausing he quietly walked up behind the boy at the piano playing "Chopsticks." He leaned over his shoulder and whispered in his ear, "Keep going. Don't stop." With that encouragement the boy began playing more vigorously. The pianist kept whispering, "Keep going. Don't stop." As he did, he reached around the boy with his right hand and began playing an improvised countermelody. He reached around with his left hand and added a bass line, all the while whispering, "Keep going. Don't stop." They ended with a flourish, to a standing ovation. The crowd—except for two chagrined parents—was unaware that this was unplanned.

The pianist is a wonderful metaphor for what the Holy Spirit does in our lives and in our ministry when we rely upon him. He takes the "Chopsticks" of our prayers and lives and turns them into a beautiful concerto, all the while encouraging us to "keep going. Don't stop." Without the Holy Spirit, our leadership is a clunky child's song. Through trusting dependence on God, prayer turns our efforts into something God makes beautiful.

The Power of the Holy Spirit Released in Prayer

Prayer is the steam engine that powered the ministry of the apostle Paul. He had learned that human effort is fruitless apart from the Spirit's anointing and empowering. There are leadership and management techniques that work in a worldly sense, but life-giving leadership is born, bathed and conducted through prayer and continual dependence on God.

This understanding did not begin with Paul but had already been characteristic of the leadership culture of the early church. To take one example from the early church, Peter had learned the power of prayer and the bankruptcy of human effort apart from God by trial and error in his time with Jesus. Early on, we see a disciple overeager to express his ideas, unable to discern between his thoughts and God's thoughts and quick to boast in his own strength. After he had been through the crucifixion of Jesus and witnessed his resurrection, Peter had been taught not to rely on his strength or wisdom but to trust and depend on God's power in the Spirit through the name of Jesus. A prime example of how much Peter had grown is seen in his reaction to the healing of the paralytic at the temple gates in Acts 3.

It was an amazing thing to see this man run and leap and praise God. Peter and John, had they not been carefully discipled, could easily have basked in the glory of this miracle, taking credit for something God had done. Sensing the rush of excitement over this spectacular event, Peter is quick to draw attention away from himself and to God's work of power: "You Israelites, why do you wonder at this, or why do you stare at us, as though by our own power or piety we had made him walk?" (Acts 3:12). Life-giving leaders understand that it is a strong tendency of our flesh, that is, our sinful nature, to give credit to human beings instead of to God. When we are functioning in the flesh and not the Spirit, we naturally think in terms of human effort and natural cause and effect. When we are functioning in the Spirit, we are fully aware that the battle is to direct all eyes on the Lord and away from human pride. So, Peter instructs them to look to the power that comes through prayer in Jesus' name: "And by faith in his name, his name itself has made this man strong, whom you see and know; and the faith that is through Jesus has given him this perfect health in the presence of all of you" (Acts 3:16).

This may seem like too rudimentary a point to make to people reading a book on Christian leadership, but my experience has led me to realize that this is a major issue in the impotence and powerlessness of the church in our culture. Professionalism has replaced prayerfulness. We have highly educated, polished leaders who all too often are prayerless and therefore spiritually powerless in their leadership and ministry. The spiritual impoverishment of the church in our culture has left us with leadership that is fleshly, focused on appearance and human effort and lacking in the Spirit-led and Spirit-empowered work that brings life, joy and salvation. Good ideas, like Peter's "Stop talking about your death like that, Jesus" (Mk 8), are shown to be demonic in origin when Jesus rebukes him with, "Get behind me, Satan! For you are setting your mind not on divine things but on human things" (Mk 8:33). This too can be said of too much activity that masquerades as ministry. It is of human origin, lacking God's anointing and empowerment. Life-giving leaders are all too aware they have a lot of good ideas *not* worth doing. They seek God's direction with deep conviction that God's ways are higher than ours, and that God's thoughts are more elevated than our plans and schemes.

The theological reason that prayer is essential for effective ministry is that prayer is an indispensable sign that God has made us his children by the Holy Spirit (Rom 8:12-27; Gal 4:6). Those who live "according to the flesh"—by their own strength, according to their own will, for their own purposes—sow "death" in their ministry (Rom 8:13). But those who are "led by the Spirit" belong to God as his children and heirs (Rom 8:14). They are the ones who have been born of the Spirit and can cry out "Abba, Father" (Rom 8:16). Those born of the Spirit are the ones who sow spiritual seeds that are harvested in life-giving ministry.

I must head off a possible misinterpretation of what I am saying here. Prayer does not displace reasoning and responsible action for Paul. But prayer is *as* essential to Paul's life as reasoning and action. He never says, "Pray, don't think." Nor does he say, as the old joke about unthinking Christians goes, "Be transformed by the removal of your minds." Instead, he affirms the renewed mind in Christ, "Be transformed by the renewing of your minds, so that you may discern what is the will of God" (Rom 12:2). But Paul's approach to ministry does stand in stark contrast with those who think and act without praying. Paul keeps a bal-

ance between praying and thinking, and so should we: "What should I
do then? I will pray with the spirit, but I will pray with the mind also; I
will sing praise with the spirit, but I will sing praise with the mind also"
(1 Cor 14:15).

Paul's is a both-and, not an either-or, choice. He prays with the mind
and in the Spirit. Graciously, when we don't know how to pray or act in
a circumstance, "the Spirit helps us in our weakness; for we do not know
how to pray as we ought, but that very Spirit intercedes with sighs too
deep for words" (Rom 8:26). As biblical theologian Oscar Cullmann
says, "It is the Holy Spirit which speaks in prayer. This is the deep truth
about prayer which we owe to the apostle."[1]

Paul's Ministry Birthed in Prayer

Paul models, from the beginning to the end of his ministry, dependence
upon God through prayer. From the beginning, Paul's missionary efforts had been birthed in prayer. Luke records how the church at Antioch received direction to anoint Paul and Barnabas for their missionary
work: "While they were worshiping the Lord and fasting, the Holy Spirit
said, 'Set apart for me Barnabas and Saul for the work to which I have
called them.' Then after fasting and praying they laid their hands on
them and sent them off. So, being sent out by the Holy Spirit, they went
down to Seleucia; and from there they sailed to Cyprus" (Acts 13:2-4).

This too was Paul's practice when he appointed leadership for the
churches he founded. He birthed ministry by prayer: "And after they
had appointed elders for them in each church, with prayer and fasting
they entrusted them to the Lord in whom they had come to believe"
(Acts 14:23). "With prayer and fasting" is the key phrase, reminiscent of
Jesus praying all night before selecting his twelve disciples.

These two examples illustrate the importance of prayer at the incep-
tion of ministry. From the beginning, every ministry needs to be birthed

and bathed in prayer. It is cliché for us to pray only when things are going wrong or when we are struggling. Life-giving leadership flows out of the direction and anointing of the Holy Spirit. We need to turn around the proverb, "Don't just sit there, do something" to "Don't just do something, sit there!" and pave the way for life-yielding ministry by praying for direction and empowerment. It is not a matter of choosing prayer over action but of sequence: pray, then do. Otherwise we end up, in the words of the old adage, asking God to fix our plans instead of yielding in advance to his guidance: "Don't ask God to bless what you are doing, but rather ask God to show you how to do what he is blessing."

Paul's Practice of Praying for Others and Asking for Personal Prayer

Prayer characterized Paul's practice from the beginning of, and throughout, his ministry. Luke again and again records his experience of the priority Paul put on prayer. Examples could be multiplied, but I offer two. When Paul was imprisoned with Silas at Philippi, he is found praying: "About midnight Paul and Silas were praying and singing hymns to God, and the prisoners were listening to them" (Acts 16:25). Upon leaving the Ephesian elders to face opposition in Jerusalem, again Luke says of Paul, "When he had finished speaking, he knelt down with them all and prayed" (Acts 20:36). We can see this same priority Paul placed upon prayer in his letters to his churches and coworkers.

We can observe Paul's conviction about the importance of prayer in how he passionately and regularly prayed for his churches. He uses words like "always," "without ceasing" and "night and day" for his pattern of prayer:

I remember you always in my prayers. (Rom 1:9; cf. Eph 1:16)

We have not ceased praying for you. (Col 1:9)

*Night and day we pray most earnestly that we may see you face to face
and restore whatever is lacking in your faith. (1 Thess 3:10; cf. 2 Tim 1:3)*

When we take into account the testimony of Luke in Acts, Paul
meant "night and day" literally. Obviously he had adapted a pattern of
prayer that he could employ wherever he was: incarcerated in a jail cell,
while working with his hands making tents, on the road as he walked,
when alone and when surrounded by others. Even Paul's disciples
picked up the crucial importance of regular prayer. So Paul can write
of Epaphras to the Colossian church: "Epaphras, who is one of you, a
servant of Christ Jesus, greets you. He is always wrestling in his prayers
on your behalf, so that you may stand mature and fully assured in everything that God wills" (Col 4:12).

It is interesting to note how Paul describes Epaphras's prayers. He
"wrestles" in prayer. Like Jacob of old, he is not content merely to
present a request to God. Epaphras engages God in prayer and intercedes for the Colossians. We can almost hear the same Jacobian spirit,
"I will not let you go until you bless them." Paul models continual
prayer and draws positive attention to one of his disciples who followed
his practice.

What did Paul pray for them? His requests ranged from practical
things like the meeting of needs, to discipleship issues like the growth
of their knowledge of the Lord, and their love for all people. At the beginning of his letter to the Ephesians, Paul writes:

*I do not cease to give thanks for you as I remember you in my prayers.
I pray that the God of our Lord Jesus Christ, the Father of glory, may
give you a spirit of wisdom and revelation as you come to know him, so
that, with the eyes of your heart enlightened, you may know what is the
hope to which he has called you, what are the riches of his glorious in-*

heritance among the saints, and what is the immeasurable greatness of his power for us who believe, according to the working of his great power. (Eph 1:16-19)

He asks for spiritual understanding of God, a kindling of the hope of the gospel, an awareness of all the blessings one obtains as a Christian and an awareness of God's immense power and strength that He employs for those who trust in him. This is revealing. The preacher and teacher Paul was completely aware that it is not human words or human reasoning that enlightens someone. It is the Spirit of God. Before Paul begins to write about other matters in the letter of Ephesians, he begins with a prayer because he knows only God can open the "eyes of the heart." This is not antirational or irrational. Rather, Paul takes seriously the relationship of spiritual revelation to rational comprehension. The Holy Spirit must reveal God if we are to understand him.

Later in the letter, Paul prays again:

I pray that, according to the riches of his glory, he may grant that you may be strengthened in your inner being with power through his Spirit, and that Christ may dwell in your hearts through faith, as you are being rooted and grounded in love. I pray that you may have the power to comprehend, with all the saints, what is the breadth and length and height and depth, and to know the love of Christ that surpasses knowledge, so that you may be filled with all the fullness of God. (Eph 3:16-19)

This is a prayer for their growth in grace. He asks for the Spirit to grant them inner strength, for Christ to dwell intimately with them through faith and for love to be their soil and foundation for all they do. He asks God to give them the ability to understand the depths of God and to know Christ's love in a full and rich way. Like the first prayer in

Ephesians, these are all things Paul writes about in the letter. But for these seeds to take root in them spiritually, Paul presses the seeds into the soil of their souls with prayer.

When he prays for his churches, he is continually thankful for what God has already done and for their response in faith, their sharing in the gospel labor and their love for one another:

> I thank my God every time I remember you, constantly praying with joy in every one of my prayers for all of you, because of your sharing in the gospel from the first day until now. (Phil 1:3-5)

> In our prayers for you we always thank God, the Father of our Lord Jesus Christ, for we have heard of your faith in Christ Jesus and of the love that you have for all the saints. (Col 1:3-4)

> We always give thanks to God for all of you and mention you in our prayers, constantly remembering before our God and Father your work of faith and labor of love and steadfastness of hope in our Lord Jesus Christ. (1 Thess 1:2-3)

God is the great deliverer and helper. He is the one who makes lasting things happen, so all praise and thankfulness is rightly directed toward him. To the Philippians, Paul writes, "Yes, and I will continue to rejoice, for I know that through your prayers and the help of the Spirit of Jesus Christ this will turn out for my deliverance" (Phil 1:18-19). God makes it happen. Prayer is how we dial into what God is doing.

Paul's practice of praying for his churches is accompanied by his habit of asking for prayer for himself and his ministry. Paul practiced partnership in his ministry. A paternalistic leader would merely stand aloof and say, "I'm praying for you," with no request for prayer, and no expressed need for help. Paul, however, sees the train of ministry traveling two ways on the tracks. It is not something he does for his churches but something he shares in with his churches. A partnership mentality characterizes his pattern of prayer, as he prays for his churches and requests prayer for himself and his coworkers.

To the Thessalonians:

Beloved, pray for us. (1 Thess 5:25)

To Philemon of the Colossians:

One thing more—prepare a guest room for me, for I am hoping through your prayers to be restored to you. (Philem 22)

To the Roman Christians—some of whom he knew and others of whom he had never met—he opens up his heart and shares his deepest concerns:

I appeal to you, brothers and sisters, by our Lord Jesus Christ and by the love of the Spirit, to join me in earnest prayer to God on my behalf, that I may be rescued from the unbelievers in Judea, and that my ministry to Jerusalem may be acceptable to the saints, so that by God's will I may come to you with joy and be refreshed in your company. (Rom 15:30-32)

He asks them to pray for the most pressing issues facing him and for the strategic issues facing his ministry. As we follow the unfolding drama at the end of the book of Acts, it becomes clear that God answers these prayers. The devious plots against Paul's life fail, and even shipwreck and snakebite cannot keep Paul from being delivered to them in Rome. Patrick Miller notes about this passage, "Here and elsewhere it is apparent that such exhortation to pray in his behalf is directly related to his mission. The prayers are always, either directly or indirectly, a prayer for his success in his mission."[2] This is an observation worth exploring further.

The Relationship of Prayer to Mission Effectiveness

E. M. Bounds ends his classic book *Prayer and Praying Men* with this conclusion: "Paul had the idea that his movements were hindered or helped by the prayers of his brethren."[3] Spiritual effects demand spiritual causes. Spirit-empowered ministry and life-giving accomplishments happen because the Holy Spirit works through yielded vessels and sometimes unyielded ones. Those who lead and minister "in the flesh" often find prayer a perfunctory function, something they do because they are supposed to, not because they feel a need. But those who have been broken of their self-will and have come to learn how God's power thrives through brokenness and surrender pray because they know they must. If God doesn't show up, then their efforts are in vain. Empowered leaders lead from a radical awareness of their dependence upon God's power.

The great British preacher of the nineteenth century, Charles Spurgeon, makes this same point:

> A certain preacher whose sermons converted many souls received
> a revelation from God that it was not his sermons or works by all
> means but the prayers of an illiterate lay brother who sat on the
> pulpit steps pleading for the success of the sermon. It may be in
> the all-revealing day so with us. We may believe after laboring
> long and wearily that all honor belongs to another builder whose
> prayers were gold, silver, and precious stones, while our sermon-
> izings being apart from prayer are but hay and stubble.[4]

Spurgeon is merely expounding what Paul modeled. He continually asked for prayer for the effectiveness of his mission. This did not decrease as he became more experienced as a minister. Throughout his ministry, Paul modeled his sense of radical dependency on God's gracious work. So he commands the Colossians:

Devote yourselves to prayer, keeping alert in it with thanksgiving. At the same time pray for us as well that God will open to us a door for the word, that we may declare the mystery of Christ, for which I am in prison, so that I may reveal it clearly, as I should. (Col 4:2-4)

To the Ephesians he says:

Pray also for me, so that when I speak, a message may be given to me to make known with boldness the mystery of the gospel, for which I am an ambassador in chains. Pray that I may declare it boldly, as I must speak. (Eph 6:19-20)

To the Thessalonians, his is consistent with his pattern:

Finally, brothers and sisters, pray for us, so that the word of the Lord may spread rapidly and be glorified everywhere, just as it is among you. (2 Thess 3:1)

After all this time as a missionary, Paul still needs to ask for prayer for an open door and a clear message. Why? Because spiritual effects need spiritual causes. As Bounds says, "The force of his request for prayer centered on him, that he might be able to talk with force, fluency, directness and courage. Paul did not depend upon his natural gifts, but on those which came to him in answer to prayer."[5]

I have worked with more than one hundred different congregations to do outreach missions over the past decade. In that work, I have seen two common mistakes that churches make with regard to mission: outreach without prayer, and prayer without outreach. The first mistake flows out of the character of the leaders of the particular congregation. If they are accustomed to ministry in the flesh, then prayer is quickly skipped over to get to the planning, goals and action. The other common mistake is much less frequent, but there are those who think that prayer substitutes for witness. Paul's ministry was birthed in prayer but lived out in front-line boldness making Jesus known to whoever would listen. Prayer does not substitute for action but births, directs and empowers that action to flow out of the Holy Spirit. "More than anyone else [Paul] shows prayer does not exclude action, but makes it fruitful in a unique way."[6] The bottom line in mission is, whatever you do will work if you pray. As Jerry Smith, a mission leader I work with, likes to say, "Always be pre-prayered."

> When Christ surveyed the crowds following Him like a leaderless mass of confused and desperate people needing every kind of help, He had compassion on them. Telling His disciples to do something about their need, He likened the crowds to a field ripe for harvest. But His first command was not to form a work crew, or plot a master grid for the fields, or dash out and start reaping. Instead, He urged them, "Ask the Lord of the harvest" (Matthew 9:38).[7]

The Imperative to Pray

From all that we have seen about Paul, we should not be surprised that he moves from his example, to teaching and exhorting his followers that they should pray, that they must pray. For those who would bear fruit for the kingdom of God, prayer is not optional. Here are six commands from across Paul's letters. Many more could be given.

Devote yourselves to prayer, keeping alert in it with thanksgiving. (Col 4:2)

Rejoice in hope, be patient in suffering, persevere in prayer. (Rom 12:12)

Pray in the Spirit at all times in every prayer and supplication. To that end keep alert and always persevere in supplication for all the saints. (Eph 6:18)

Rejoice always, pray without ceasing, give thanks in all circumstances; for this is the will of God in Christ Jesus for you. (1 Thess 5:16-18)

First of all, then, I urge that supplications, prayers, intercessions, and thanksgivings be made for everyone. . . . I desire, then, that in every place the men should pray, lifting up holy hands without anger or argument. (1 Tim 2:1, 8)

Do not worry about anything, but in everything by prayer and supplication with thanksgiving let your requests be made known to God. (Phil 4:6)

We need prayerlessness to cease among church leaders. Our world is groaning and longing for the kingdom of God to be revealed. Paul commands us to pray continually, to pray about all things and to do everything in a trusting attitude of prayer.

Persistence Needed: Ministry Is a Spiritual Battle

Paul teaches that we should pray "always" and "without ceasing." These commands recur often in his letters.[8] Why is there such a need for prayer? In addition to spiritual effects needing spiritual causes, there is also an understanding that there exists continuous spiritual opposition to Spirit-empowered work. Not only is there pushback from human opponents, but also there is targeted opposition from dark spiritual beings and forces:

Finally, be strong in the Lord and in the strength of his power. Put on the whole armor of God, so that you may be able to stand against the wiles of the devil. For our struggle is not against enemies of blood and flesh, but against the rulers, against the authorities, against the cosmic powers of this present darkness, against the spiritual forces of evil in the heavenly places. Therefore take up the whole armor of God, so that you may be able to withstand on that evil day, and having done everything, to stand firm. Stand therefore, and fasten the belt of truth around your waist, and put on the breastplate of righteousness. As shoes for your feet put on whatever will make you ready to proclaim the gospel of peace. With all of these, take the shield of faith, with which you will be able to quench all the flaming arrows of the evil one. Take the helmet of salvation, and the sword of the Spirit, which is the word of God. Pray in the Spirit at all times in every prayer and supplication. To that end keep alert and always persevere in supplication for all the saints. (Eph 6:10-18)

It is popular in our day to dismiss such references as quaint and to "reinterpret" what Paul is saying to exclude the existence of a literal devil or demonic opposition.[9]

To such revisionists, C. S. Lewis's words, over a half-century old, still have a sharp edge:

There are two equal and opposite errors into which our race can fall about the devils. One is to disbelieve in their existence. The other is to believe, and to feel an excessive and unhealthy interest in them. They themselves are equally pleased by both errors, and hail a materialist or a magician with the same delight.[10]

Much more recently, Francis MacNutt, a pastor experienced in spiritual deliverance and married to a psychotherapist, says,

Ministers of the Gospel need to stop passing the buck by denying that demonic oppression exists or by simply referring people to psychiatrists or counselors when what is needed is deliverance. Counseling and medication may also be needed; and we should by all means cooperate with mental health professionals. But ministers must not continue to deny responsibility *in their own field.*[11]

My own experience is this. In the early phase of my ministry, three things were true: I mostly did ministry in the flesh, I saw little abiding spiritual fruit, and I was completely unaware of the tricks of the devil that kept me from moving in spiritual authority. Much later, as a result of moving to front-line evangelism as the focus of my ministry, all three of these changed dramatically. Through God's gracious breaking I began dying to ministry in the flesh. With my ego more out of the way, I began seeing significant spiritual fruit. And like it or not (mostly, I didn't like it), I became aware of fierce spiritual warfare going on around me to thwart what God wanted done. I wasn't looking for a fight. But, when my ministry began to be a threat to the kingdom of darkness, then and there I began experiencing dark spiritual backlash.

The left-brain rationalist in me could no longer ignore the scriptural teaching on the spiritual opposition that inevitably comes to those who are following Jesus. I began to realize that warfare prayer is a crucial leadership activity. If it is left to the side, then no spiritual ground is gained and no significant ministry moves forward. This may sound harsh, but I now believe that those who do not believe in a literal devil or who never experience spiritual attack probably are doing ministry in the flesh and are therefore no threat to the kingdom of darkness.

Prayer is the main weapon we are given to do spiritual warfare. "Indeed, we live as human beings, but we do not wage war according to human standards; for the weapons of our warfare are not merely human, but they have divine power to destroy strongholds" (2 Cor 10:3-4). This is why Jesus taught, and Paul modeled, our "need to pray always and not to lose heart" (Lk 18:1).

Fortunately, when we walk with Christ we are enrolled in the school of prayer.[12] He uses the disasters, humiliations, failures, betrayals and breakings that come our way in positions of leadership to break our false pride, to crucify our self-will and to teach us the gift of radical dependence on God. We, like his disciples, can ask him to teach us to pray. Grace abounds. When we do not know how to pray as we should, his Holy Spirit intercedes for us according to God's will (Rom 8:26-27). And even when we have been prayerless, Jesus still "always lives to make intercession" for us (Heb 7:25). Whenever and however we pray, "let us therefore approach the throne of grace with boldness, so that we may receive mercy and find grace to help in time of need" (Heb 4:16).

Questions for Reflection and Discussion

1. Reflect and discuss: "The question is not: How many people take you seriously: How much are you going to accomplish? Can you show some results? But: Are you in love with Jesus? Perhaps another way of putting the question would be: Do you know the incarnate God?" (Henri Nouwen, *In the Name of Jesus* [New York: Crossroad, 1990], p. 24).

2. Evaluate your calendar over the last three months. How many gatherings, apart from your regular worship time, have you and your leaders had for the purpose of prayer? How many business meetings have you had in that same period of time?

3. Do you pray for your ministry and messages, or do you merely plan and perform them?

4. Be candid with yourself. Do you observe God moving in your ministry? How does that relate to your prayerfulness or lack thereof?

5. Is there any unexplained pushback or spiritual opposition to your ministry? What do you attribute this to?

6. Reflect and discuss: "When Christians have meetings, the devil smiles. When Christians make great plans, the devil laughs. When Christians pray, the devil trembles" (Corrie ten Boom).

8

THE RACE
TO THE BOTTOM

*Servant leadership is merely the application
of the dynamic of the gospel to the task of leadership.*

KLYNE SNODGRASS

*For God's foolishness is wiser than human wisdom, and God's
weakness is stronger than human strength.*

*Consider your own call, brothers and sisters: not many of you were wise
by human standards, not many were powerful, not many were of noble
birth. But God chose what is foolish in the world to shame the wise; God
chose what is weak in the world to shame the strong; God chose what is
low and despised in the world, things that are not, to reduce to nothing
things that are, so that no one might boast in the presence of God.*

1 CORINTHIANS 1:25-29

Every child is different. Our youngest daughter was quite
strong-willed when she was small (a characteristic that has softened only
a little!). She has always known what she wants and where she is going.
My wife, Ingrid, has always found this a challenge, since she herself is
tenderhearted, a lover, not a fighter. Conflict is the bane of her existence.

Once, when our daughter was about three, she was locked in a mortal combat of the wills with my wife. Exasperated, Ingrid blurted out to her, "You just want to be the mom and the boss." As if she had contemplated this question before, our daughter calmly replied, "No, I just want to be the boss."

That same person lives in all of us. Our sinful side, the self-will Paul calls the flesh, is the part of us that wants to be in control. The original temptation in the Garden of Eden was to overstep, to overreach, to wrest control away from God and take it to ourselves. Somewhere deep down inside us we all just want to be the boss and to be on top. To take a recent glaring example, heavyweight boxer Evander Holyfield has not applied the theology of the cross to his life. Discussing his comeback he wrongly claims, "God don't want me to go out on the bottom end. He wants me to go out on the top end. I know that."[1] How does he know that? It does not come from the New Testament. This desire itself reflects our darkness, not the light of God working in our lives. To exercise Spirit-anointed leadership we must confront head-on this specter of our souls.

Bottom Up, Not Top Down

Paul's paradigm for advanced Christian leadership is not being a boss but serving as a slave. Spirit-led leadership is not about towering in power over others but about stooping low in submitted service. North American translations of the Bible mostly gloss over the slavery imagery of the New Testament by choosing the English words "serve," "service" and "servant" where "slave" and "slavery" were intended. Most readers of North American translations are surprised to learn that the New Testament uses some 191 words for the institution of slavery in the original Greek. Paul's favorite self-characterization is some form of "slave of Christ."[2] Even when he calls himself "apostle" he has this in mind, since apostles were usually slaves who could be sent on perilous journeys because they were expendable. Moreover, he commonly refers to Jesus as *kyrios*, which would be heard by Greek-speakers as "master of a slave" as much as "divine Lord." This was their common experience throughout the Roman Empire, where one-third of the population was slaves (*douloi*), one-third masters (*kyrioi*) and one-third former slaves or freedmen.[3] In this cultural context, Paul portrays following Jesus as living as slave of our Lord and Master: "For whoever was called in the Lord as a slave is a freed person belonging to the Lord, just as whoever was free when called is a slave of Christ. You were bought with a price; do not become slaves of human masters" (1 Cor 7:22-23).

This is not just for leaders. This is what it means to be a follower of Jesus. We were redeemed, that is, "bought with a price," from slavery to sin. We were freed when we became slaves of Jesus. The inherent tension in the imagery that we are slave and free reflects the tension we experience as conflicted people who have been made alive in the Spirit but still limp along with our sin nature.

Paul's teaching about discipleship as slavery to the Lord came from Jesus. In Matthew 20:20-28 Jesus gives us a clear, countercultural picture for our exercise of authority when he confronts his disciples' desire to sit at the head of the table.

Zebedee's wife was thinking of her sons when she kneeled before Jesus and begged him, "Declare that these two sons of mine will sit, one at your right hand and one at your left, in your kingdom" (Mt 20:21). I suppose she was doing nothing different than any parent who has ever lobbied to get their child a privileged opportunity. But Jesus connects her and her sons' desire to be seated at the place of honor and authority with a manner of relating to others that exalts oneself and subjugates others. So, to all of the disciples Jesus said, "You know that the rulers of the Gentiles lord it over them, and their great ones are tyrants over them. It will not be so among you" (Mt 20:25-26). We all want to be the boss, but Jesus makes it clear that in his kingdom: *It will not be so among you*. These are Jesus' seven last words on whether or not we are to exercise Christian leadership in the way the world leverages authority. Inside us somewhere is the dictum, "My way is Yahweh." Lords and tyrants aren't just aberrations of history—they are the normal stuff of the human psyche. *It will not be so among you*.

Jesus goes on to turn worldly understanding of authority, honor and power on its head. In the upside-down kingdom, leaders—followers of Jesus—reflect the great social reversal that Jesus initiates. So Jesus gives his radical directive for would-be leaders: "but whoever wishes to be great among you must be your servant (*diakonos*), and whoever wishes to be first among you must be your slave (*doulos*); just as the Son of Man came not to be served but to serve, and to give his life a ransom for many" (Mt 20:26-28).

This teaching orders a hierarchy, but one that is from the bottom up rather than the top down. Jesus says that whoever wants to be second greatest should seek to serve. But first among the great are those who are "slaves"—their lives are patterned after their master, Jesus. The race is not to the top, where the power and prestige are. The race, for followers of Jesus, is to the bottom where humility, surrender and service are to be found.

We must face the side of us that wants to be in charge and call it what it is: darkness. Following Jesus means dying to this demonic aspect of our beings and living to be a servant like Jesus is. When we lord it over others, we avoid the cost of following Jesus. But when we make ourselves vulnerable by yielding up control, we trust God's sovereignty to bring his good out of whatever may come. This leap from lording to service and surrender puts us in a position of radical dependence and trust in God. We come to rely on God's will and purpose—even if it includes suffering. We no longer think, "My way is Yahweh," but, "Whatever you want, Lord!"

Go Low

Most of my Christian life my father was opposed to spiritual things and discussing God. It was long one of the most painful parts of my daily life. The thing I most wanted to do was to share Jesus with him. He never wanted to talk about Jesus. A few years ago he ended up in the hospital with a series of major health issues that ended up taking his life. After one of his stays in intensive care, I flew to California to see him. All the way there I prayed and hoped that I would have a chance to present the gospel to him and to see him receive Jesus into his life.

When I got there, he was as gruff as usual. Soon after I walked into his room he barked, "Get me some Epsom salt to soak my feet." He had been a printer his whole life, and one of his regular pleasures was coming home after a day on his feet and soaking them in Epsom salt. I dutifully trudged to the nurses' station certain this wasn't going to happen. When his nurse was resistant (we weren't even sure he could sit up), I persisted since I found it easier to buck her than my father. She caved to my pressure and gave me two plastic containers that I held up to my feet and realized his feet would barely fit into. I returned to his room, filled the containers with warm water and helped him sit up.

Immediately I realized that it would be impossible for him to soak his feet by himself, so I grabbed a rag, stooped down and gently put his feet in the containers and squeezed water over the top of his feet. As the water overflowed and drenched the knees of my dress slacks, I knelt there complaining to God that all I wanted to do was share him with my dad. How come there never seemed to be an opening? In that moment, with my dad staring at the back of my neck, I felt the Holy Spirit nudge me to an awareness that what I was doing was *exactly* what my father needed to "hear." Quite unplanned on my part and without using words, my father heard that I loved and cared for him, and he saw a picture of the servant Jesus, in spite of me. I never got a chance to verbally share the gospel with him that day, but a breakthrough had happened for him and for me. A few weeks later my friend and then my sister told him about the love and forgiveness he could have through Jesus. He asked the Lord into his life, and we baptized him in the hospital.

It was only upon reflection that I realized this is what Jesus meant when he confronted Zebedee's sons and their mother. All you have to do is go low. That is how leadership is done on Jesus' team. If they hadn't figured it out from his explicit teaching, Jesus models this very thing for them when he washed their feet later on. If I felt humbled washing my father's feet, it would be nothing like the social stigma of washing someone's feet in the ancient world. This was considered the most shameful part of the body, and only the lowliest servant would be assigned this humiliating task. That's why Peter couldn't endure Jesus belittling himself this way. But Jesus lowers himself to paint a lucid leadership picture with his own countercultural actions:

> *Jesus, knowing that the Father had given all things into his hands, and that he had come from God and was going to God, got up from the table, took off his outer robe, and tied a towel around himself. Then he poured water into a basin and began to wash the disciples' feet and to wipe them with the towel that was tied around him. He came to Simon Peter, who said to him, "Lord, are you going to wash my feet?" Jesus answered, "You do not know now what I am doing, but later you will understand." Peter said to him, "You will never wash my feet." Jesus answered, "Unless I wash you, you have no share with me. . . . "*

*After he had washed their feet, had put on his robe, and had returned
to the table, he said to them, "Do you know what I have done to you?
You call me Teacher and Lord—and you are right, for that is what I
am. So if I, your Lord and Teacher, have washed your feet, you also
ought to wash one another's feet. For I have set you an example, that
you also should do as I have done to you. Very truly, I tell you, servants
are not greater than their master, nor are messengers greater than the
one who sent them. If you know these things, you are blessed if you do
them." (Jn 13:3-17)*

Jesus just had been given "all things into his hands" (Jn 13:3). He had
arrived. The temptation would have been great to act puffed up, to show
off a little and to let people around know whose company they were
keeping. At least, that's how sinful souls deal with power and prestige.
But, as if to put an exclamation point on his earlier teaching, Jesus models *It shall not be so with you:* "I have set you an example, that you also
should do as I have done to you. . . . If you know these things, you are
blessed if you do them" (Jn 13:15, 17).

Don't Worry About Getting Up

Jesus portrays the path to anointed leadership: "You are blessed if you"
humble yourself and wash feet like he did. Theologically Paul places
this downward movement into a larger picture of how God works in
Philippians 2:5-11:

*Let the same mind be in you that was in Christ Jesus, who, though
he was in the form of God, did not regard equality with God as something to be exploited, but emptied himself, taking the form of a slave,
being born in human likeness. And being found in human form, he
humbled himself and became obedient to the point of death—even
death on a cross. Therefore God also highly exalted him and gave*

him the name that is above every name, so that at the name of Jesus
every knee should bend, in heaven and on earth and under the earth,
and every tongue should confess that Jesus Christ is Lord, to the glory
of God the Father.

Jesus' humility in service reflects his larger, cosmic self-humbling of
surrendering his privileged position in heaven and coming down as a
human being. But he goes lower still: he is obedient, even to the point
of dying on a cross. It was culturally shocking for the disciples to experience Jesus washing their feet. His crucifixion was way beyond that.
They abandoned him because they could not process this traumatic
event. It was emotionally distressful because of the gory physical torture
and public humiliation of dying naked in front of everyone. But it dis-
turbed them more deeply than this, since they had been taught that,
"anyone hung on a tree is under God's curse" (Deut 21:23; cf. Gal 3:13).

Crucifixion is not the end of the story. It is merely the end of an early
scene in the larger drama that follows a striking down-up pattern. Jesus
expands the principle to "All we have to do is go low. We don't have to
worry about getting up. God will raise us up." Obedience yields vindi-
cation, but in God's time and in God's way. Because he humbled himself in obedience, "therefore God also highly exalted him and gave him
the name that is above every name" (Phil 2:9).

Paul begins his citation of this hymn with the exhortation that we
should think this same way. This was clearly Paul's practice of ministry.
He goes on to portray his own race to the bottom as leader in the next
chapter:

I, too, have reason for confidence in the flesh. If anyone else has reason
to be confident in the flesh, I have more: circumcised on the eighth day,
a member of the people of Israel, of the tribe of Benjamin, a Hebrew
born of Hebrews; as to the law, a Pharisee; as to zeal, a persecutor of

the church; as to righteousness under the law, blameless. Yet whatever
gains I had, these I have come to regard as loss because of Christ. More
than that, I regard everything as loss because of the surpassing value of
knowing Christ Jesus my Lord. For his sake I have suffered the loss of
all things, and I regard them as rubbish, in order that I may gain
Christ. (Phil 3:4-8)

From the time he met the risen Jesus on the road to Damascus, Paul
regularly "went low." Gentiles became his main mission, an issue that
continually brought him opposition and physical persecution. Paul hu-
miliated himself to befriend such outsiders. Furthermore, he associated
with women and slaves, seeking out those at the bottom rungs of society
instead of cloistering himself with the elite. He refused the financial patronage of the powerful (see 1 Cor 9), and worked with his own hands—
a social stigma for any who wanted to run in the circles of high society.

It is cliché for some pastoral leaders to be known to socialize with the
well-heeled and to neglect those who may need their companionship
most. Going high is the worldly thing to do, but Jesus condemned it:
"Woe to you Pharisees! For you love to have the seat of honor in the syn-
agogues and to be greeted with respect in the marketplaces" (Lk 11:43).
People notice how much interest the leader takes in his or her security,
salary, pension and benefits. A whole generation is upon us who have
no respect for leaders who look to their own interests first and neglect
the needs all around them. To lead Jesus' way means to live on the edge,
at the bottom where there is little power or prestige or security. All we
have to do is go low. We don't have to worry about getting up. God will
lift us up.

Henri Nouwen was an accomplished Harvard professor and Catholic priest who understood this dynamic. For the final phase of his ministry, he left the ivy towers to serve in a residential facility for the

developmentally disabled. It was as low as he could find to go, and yet he testified to the incredible ways he found God touching him through the friends he made there. He summarizes his reflections on his race to the bottom this way:

> I am deeply convinced that the Christian leader of the future is called to be completely irrelevant and to stand in this world with nothing to offer but his or her own vulnerable self. That is the way Jesus came to reveal God's love. The great message that we have to carry, as ministers of God's word and followers of Jesus, is that God loves us not because of what we do or accomplish, but because God has created and redeemed us in love and has chosen us to proclaim that love as the source of all human life.[4]

Questions for Reflection and Discussion

1. Think of an example of a leader you know who has gone low, and describe the spiritual fruit he or she bore.

2. When you think of surrendering power, security and prestige, what would you have to give up? How does it feel?

3. Reflect on the principle, "All we have to do is go low. We don't have to worry about getting up. God will raise us up." What is your reaction?

4. When you claimed Jesus as your Lord, you yielded to him the authority to pattern your steps and direct your life. What elements of your life need to more fully reflect your surrender to the Lord Jesus?

5. Are the leaders of your church or ministry known as being the elite, or are they known for their sacrificial service and humility?

One recent Christian book on leadership is called *The Ascent of a Leader*.[5] In light of Jesus' teaching in Matthew 20 and John 13 and his example in Philippians 2, how would you assess this title?

9

THE LEADERSHIP
WE NEED IS
APOSTOLIC

It is too small a thing for you to be my servant
to restore the tribes of Jacob
and bring back those of Israel I have kept.
I will also make you a light for the Gentiles,
that you may bring my salvation to the ends of the earth.

ISAIAH 49:6 NIV

For I will not venture to speak of anything except what Christ has
accomplished through me to win obedience from the Gentiles,
by word and deed, by the power of signs and wonders, by the power
of the Spirit of God, so that from Jerusalem and as far around as
Illyricum I have fully proclaimed the good news of Christ.
Thus I make it my ambition to proclaim the good news, not where
Christ has already been named, so that I do not build on someone else's
foundation, but as it is written, "Those who have never been told of him
shall see, and those who have never heard of him shall understand."

ROMANS 15:18-21

The church exists by mission as a fire exists by burning.
EMIL BRUNNER

THE LEADERSHIP WE NEED TODAY IS apostolic leadership. *Apostolic* means embodying New Testament Christianity's DNA. This book has been about how we need to actualize New Testament principles in our churches and ministries today. Apostolic leaders are those who understand, embody and employ New Testament Christianity in their teaching and by their example. We do not need more glorified managers. We need Spirit-anointed leaders.

> If you have apostolic passion, you are one of the most dangerous people on the planet. The world no longer rules your heart. You are no longer seduced by getting and gaining but devoted to spreading and proclaiming the glory of God in the nations. You live as a pilgrim, unattached to the cares of this world. You are not afraid of loss. You even dare to believe you may be given the privilege of dying to spread his fame on the earth. The Father's passions have become your passions. You find your satisfaction and significance in him. You believe he is with you always, to the end of life itself. You are sold out to God, and you live for the Lamb. Satan fears you, and the angels applaud you. Your greatest dream is that his name will be praised in languages never before heard in heaven. Your reward is the look of pure delight you anticipate seeing in his eyes when you lay at his feet and the just reward of his suffering: the worship of the redeemed.[1]

The reason that apostolic leaders are needed in North America is because we are a mission field. The day of the local church is over—the day of the mission station outpost is here. To reiterate what I wrote in the opening chapter, we are now the fifth most unchurched nation on the planet. Only China, India, Indonesia and Russia have more non-Christians than we do. Conservatively, China has 150 million Christians to our 95 million (a generous estimate of American Christians). If we look at specific groups, portions of our nation are almost completely without the gospel. For example, deaf people in our country are 98 percent un-churched. Those under age twenty-five match this need for evangeliza-tion. The past decade has seen a decline in the number of evangelical Christians. Though many groups claim gains, the vast majority of gains tend to be transfer members, sheep shuffled from one group to another. Overall, the Christian "market share" has diminished.[2]

The past few generations of North American Christianity have been marked by "come" strategies of mission. That is, the explicit strategy for evangelism for churches is usually a version of "If they come to our church, then we will be hospitable and outgoing toward them." If a church does attempt a more assertive form of outreach, this often means a marketing strategy, an advertising campaign that nine times out of ten is focused on people who are already Christians looking for a church. Most ministry and leadership in our culture are *not* apostolic. A com-mon comment among missiologists is that "the North American church is the most dysfunctional church in the world."

To be apostolic means to understand that we are sent to spread the good news of Jesus and his kingdom. An apostle is literally "one who is sent." The "sent" nature of the church is reflected in "go" strategies of mission, which reflect God's apostolic nature. Seeing the world's des-perate need to be salvaged from sin, God sent his Son. When the Son was raised up from the earth, he sent the Holy Spirit to be our guide and counselor. The Jewish people were blessed to be a blessing and were sent to be a light to the nations: "It is too small a thing for you to be my servant / to restore the tribes of Jacob / and bring back those of Israel I have kept. / I will also make you a light for the Gentiles, / that you may bring my salvation to the ends of the earth" (Is 49:6 NIV). So also, in his

last and guiding command to the church, Jesus said, "Go." Apostolic
leaders have worshiped a sending God and have heard his command to
go. They lead the church out of the comfort of the Christian ghetto into
the heartbeat of God among a broken and hurting world. As the author
of Hebrews says, our ministry is to reflect the work of Jesus: "Therefore
Jesus also suffered outside the city gate in order to sanctify the people by
his own blood. Let us then go to him outside the camp and bear the
abuse he endured" (Heb 13:12-13). How the church in our land needs to
be led "outside the camp" of the comfortable to share Jesus with those
who need him so desperately!

The Stained-Glass Barrier

Many churched people seem unaware of how irrelevant and obscure
Christianity seems to the majority of not-yet Christians all around us.
The majority of citizens in our country may have never heard the name
of Jesus used in a reverent way. They never go to church, never listen to
Christian radio, never buy Christian music and never frequent a Christian bookstore, concert or seminar. However they might describe it, to
them the church has sent out a force field, an invisible message that
they are unwanted. Much of the church, by contrast, seems to believe
(if actions are any reflection of belief), that lost people should be able
to find their way to church. If not, too bad for them.

Garrison Keillor, with tongue in cheek, describes the "Dark Lutherans" of his imaginary town of Lake Wobegon. They could easily describe much of nonapostolic Christianity that is so evident in the visible
church in the United States today:

The Dark Lutherans held the Truth, and thus were rejected by the
world, and their isolation was proof of their righteousness. They
sang:

The gift to be righteous is the gift to say no,
And depart from the place you should not go,
Renouncing the company of unclean souls,
And thus we are added to the saintly rolls.
Deny, deny, shall be our delight,
And by separation to come out right,
And wait for the day when we all shall die
And find true fellowship by and by.[3]

This kind of church is like those religious folks whom Jesus reacted so strongly against because they complained that he was cavorting with "tax collectors and sinners" (Lk 15). He was so irritated by this complaint that he tells three parables to describe God's nature and his passionate pursuit of lost people. The good Shepherd leaves the ninety-nine in search of the one lost sheep. The woman who loses a coin turns the house upside down in search until she finds it. The gracious and generous father sits waiting on the porch for his son to come home from eating with the pigs. God is a seeking God. He searches until he finds. He does not leave us in a ditch but comes and helps us out. As he has done, so we are to do also.

The stained-glass barrier principle of mission understanding is that many people will never hear the gospel if they have to come to church to hear it. That is because there is a strong nonverbal message they receive that warns them they are not welcome. If they are going to hear the gospel, someone must go to their world and speak to them in words they can understand. God is a sending God. He has commanded us to go so that they will not be left in their sins. Many Christian ministries in our culture are like football teams that huddle continually but never take a snap and never move the ball down the field. While we wait placidly for people to come to our churches, God's command and commission stand: Go into the world!

The Leadership We Need Must Be Grown

The leadership we need must be grown, cultivated, mentored and pruned. There are many apostolic networks that have sprung up and are raising up apostolic leadership. Still, for too many, life is lived in a contemporary version of the medieval model that focuses on buildings and clergy. Then it was the cathedral and chapel, bishop and priest. Now it is the church building, pastor and staff. For many churchgoers, all they have known is an academic/spectator form of Christianity. The pastor is the trained lecturer, and the congregants are supposed to be good listeners and put their money in the offering plate. In some ways this academic/spectator model is a reflection of the seminaries that have trained the pastors. The duty of seminarians being trained is to listen, do what they are told and pay their money for the privilege.

If we understand that we are truly on the mission field, then we operate in a completely different way. We no longer look for secular qualifications for leaders such as a particular academic degree. Rather, we focus on personal character, spiritual gifting, God's calling, on-the-job equipping and demonstrated effectiveness in ministry. It is common to hear pastors calmly describe how long it took them to overcome their seminary training. That is because seminary training is *not* focused on leadership development, and this is coming from a man who has taught at two really good seminaries. The old adage applies here: insanity is doing the same things over and over and expecting to get different results.

Apostolic principles cannot be learned in the bunker of seminary but must be absorbed on the front line of mission. Apostolic leadership is released when we recognize giftings, affirm callings, and equip and engage emerging leaders in the work of mission and ministry so they can learn on the job. Is there a place for seminary training? Many still think so. But 80 percent of churches being planted in our country are being planted by nonseminary graduates. A study of more than a thousand churches on five continents has demonstrated that there is an inverse relationship between healthy churches and seminary-trained leaders. That is, healthy churches tend to have nonseminary trained leaders.[4] The comeback to this observation is sometimes, "But we need pastors who are doctrinally trained." What evidence is there that seminary education equips a pastor to be orthodox? Many of the most well-endowed and prestigious seminaries in our country are the seedbeds of contemporary abandonment of classical Christianity. Many pastors learn there just enough to make them less than effective the rest of their ministries. There is a causal relationship between how we have been training leaders in seminary and the demise of Christian mission in our land.

Because of their training, many established leaders who have come up through this model of church may not be able to reproduce apostolic leadership. They may feel comfortable in their study, at committee meetings and leading worship services, but they readily feel out of their depth in sharing Jesus with a not-yet Christian who is their next-door neighbor. Many trained leaders have not led another person to Christ in years (if ever), and many have no significant relationship with a not-yet Christian with whom they could share Jesus if they wanted to. We do not need good committee members or lecturers. We need anointed teachers and role models who demonstrate for us how to be Jesus to the hurting, lost and lonely people who populate our land.

Whatever You Want, Lord!

A few years ago I was a part of a team of about 150 people working with ten churches in the Los Angeles area to reach not-yet Christians in their neighborhoods. There were about ten of us on the oversight team, sleeping on the floor in an empty apartment for the week. Even though most of the day our oversight team was out among the other team members, in the mornings and evenings we started to have an effect on those around us in the apartment complex where we were staying. They heard us singing, saw us reading our Bibles and knew something odd was happening.

Early every morning there was a young Mexican man who left for work and then returned late. We started to develop some rapport with him as the week developed, and he always seemed eager to greet us even though he spoke little English and our Spanish was not much more developed. Near the end of the week, one night he and three other people knocked on our door carrying some six packs of soda. We invited them in thinking, "Ah, God has given us an opportunity to minister to these folks." As it turned out, they were all Christians, and they had come to find out how God was answering their prayers for us and to encourage us in the Lord. They had moved to this apartment complex from Mexico to be missionaries to the Spanish-speaking people of that area. We shared some wonderful fellowship, and then we asked them how we could pray for them.

They were reluctant to ask for prayer, but finally the first one said, "¡Lo que tu quieres, Señor!" "Whatever you want, Lord!" We pressed for more, but that was his only request. In humility and surrender he had come from Mexico. He worked long hours as a laborer, his tent making so he could be God's apostle to that area. In humility and trust he knew what to ask for in prayer—what does God want? We asked the second man, and his request in Spanish was the same as the first: "Whatever God wants!" The third and the fourth were the same.

We joined hands and prayed for them with joyful and thankful hearts, asking that God would have his way with them and direct them and keep them in his will. When we had prayed, they too lifted up prayers, anointed and powerful, for the work we were doing. I picked up most of what they prayed and knew they were communing with the Father they knew very intimately. Then they left.

When they left, we all realized that we had been visited by messengers from God to us. These messengers embodied the apostolic DNA that we so desperately need in our land. They were humble and surrendered, focusing on following Master Jesus. They paid the price and labored tirelessly to obey his will. They were prayerful and fruitful, raising up disciples who could raise up disciples. They knew all about the race to the bottom. Like Jesus, they surrendered themselves, went low and found God using them in powerful ways. May God raise up apostolic leaders like them for our nation.

Appendix

HEARING GOD'S DIRECTION FOR YOUR MINISTRY

A compelling burden is laid upon me by God; for woe is me unless I proclaim the good news about Jesus.

1 CORINTHIANS 9:16

And now, bound and compelled by the Spirit, I go to Jerusalem, not knowing what awaits me there.

ACTS 20:22

WHEN WE ARE SEEKING DIRECTION for the future, for our lives and our ministries, how does this work itself out? To accomplish spiritual results we do not create the future by visioning it or by mobilizing people to create our picture of what the future will be. I am directly criticizing a predominant teaching among Christian writing and leadership seminars that promote the importance of vision. My criticism of them is they do not use "vision" the way the Bible does, and their teaching tends to promote flesh acts, not Spirit-led leadership. By contrast, in this appendix I will focus on Paul's spiritual understanding of burden, a slave's ob-

ligation to his Master to fulfill his Master's wishes. This is the language
that Paul uses and the pattern that he exemplifies in his leadership.

From Driven to Burdened

From an early age, Paul was a driven person. By the time he had
reached maturity, you might call him purpose-driven. His vision was to
uphold the Jewish religion and to obliterate the emerging threat of
Christian believers. At his first appearance in the historical record, he
stands approvingly, watching the coats of those who slaughtered
Stephen with stones because of his belief in Jesus as Lord (Acts 7:58–
8:1).

From there Paul, "was ravaging the church." He systematically and
ruthlessly went from house to house in order to live out his purpose and
fulfill his vision of dismantling the fledgling Christian threat to his heritage and religion (Acts 8:3). Ironically, before he was even a Christian,
Paul was already serving God's greater purpose by scattering and driving
out the Christians: "Now those who were scattered went from place to
place, proclaiming the word" (Acts 8:4). Though he was unaware of it,
Paul was playing for the other team, fulfilling the plans of the One who
would soon confront him and convert him on the road to Damascus.

Paul, up to that time known as Saul, stayed on this laser-beam focus
until his face-to-face confrontation with Jesus:

> *Meanwhile Saul, still breathing threats and murder against the disci-
> ples of the Lord, went to the high priest and asked him for letters to the
> synagogues at Damascus, so that if he found any who belonged to the
> Way, men or women, he might bring them bound to Jerusalem. Now
> as he was going along and approaching Damascus, suddenly a light
> from heaven flashed around him. He fell to the ground and heard a
> voice saying to him, "Saul, Saul, why do you persecute me?" He asked,*

"Who are you, Lord?" The reply came, "I am Jesus, whom you are per-
secuting. But get up and enter the city, and you will be told what you
are to do." The men who were traveling with him stood speechless, be-
cause they heard the voice but saw no one. Saul got up from the
ground, and though his eyes were open, he could see nothing; so they
led him by the hand and brought him into Damascus. For three days
he was without sight, and neither ate nor drank." (Acts 9:1-9)

From this point on, Paul's life was radically changed, reflected by the
change from his Hebrew name Saul to his Greco-Roman name Paul.
He would ever look back to this crucial turning point in his life. His
whole ministry would be marked by this event. From here on Paul felt
owned, called and compelled by Christ. He continually and crisply ar-
ticulated his life purpose and personal mission: "I am Christ's apostle to
the Gentiles." For him, this revelatory vision of Jesus on the Damascus
road had charted the course for the rest of his entire life and preaching.[1]

Paul saw this as the day he got tagged as Christ's slave. In a revealing
passage at the end of Galatians, Paul makes references to the "slave tat-
toos of Jesus" that he carried on his body (*stigmata Iēsou*, Gal 6:17). This
cryptic comment can be understood as the physical scars and deformities Paul bore because of the persecutions he endured. But it is possible
to interpret this more specifically as scars around his eyes that he received as a result of his blinding on the road to Damascus. This may explain why Paul had to write so large (Gal 6:11), and why the Galatian
Christians would have "plucked out their eyes and given them to" Paul
if they could have (Gal 4:15).[2]

Paul uses master-slave imagery to address his Spirit-given compulsion to spread the message about Jesus: "A slave's obligation is laid upon
me by God; for woe is me unless I proclaim the good news about Jesus"
(1 Cor 9:16). The word I have translated here "slave's obligation" is the

Greek word *anankē*. It expresses the loss of one's right of self-determination and the absolute compulsion a slave had to do whatever his or her master bid (remember: the Greek word for "Lord" is the same word for a slave's "master," *kyrios*).[3] To Philemon Paul says he is not simply a "prisoner" but "a prisoner of Christ Jesus" (Philem 1). This imagery appears again and again in Paul's letters as he often refers to himself as Christ's slave, compelled and dragged about the empire to proclaim Jesus' love and power.[4] To illustrate, he introduces himself to the Christians in Rome as "Paul, a slave of Christ Jesus, called apostle, set apart for the gospel of God" (Rom 1:1). He reminds the Corinthians, "For we do not preach ourselves, but Jesus Christ as Master (*kyrios*), and ourselves as your slaves on account of Jesus" (2 Cor 4:5). To the Galatians, he writes a direct and clear description of his self-understanding, "For now am I seeking to please people or God? If I still were seeking to please people, Christ's slave I would not be!" (Gal 1:10). To the Philippians, he introduces himself and Timothy as workers who share a submission to their master Jesus, "Paul and Timothy, slaves of Christ Jesus, to all the holy ones in Christ Jesus" (Phil 1:1). To Titus, he links his apostleship to the nations with his obligation to his master, "Paul, slave of God, apostle of Jesus Christ" (Tit 1:1).

Paul's missionary journeys were not laid out on some master plan or AAA trip planner but were his Master's plan unfolded to him piece by piece along the way. Paul did not have an organizational plan or a ten-year vision. His direction seemed focused and occasional: now he's crossing over to Macedonia, now heading to Jerusalem. Now he's heading to Rome, but he is convinced God wants him to head on to Spain. He was compelled, pushed and led forward by his sense of ownership by Jesus, who had tagged him on the Damascus Road. This was Paul's burden, his deep compulsion—and, I think, deep desire—to do what his Master, the Lord Jesus, wanted him to do.

Pray for a Burden

I am well aware that much of the leadership literature promotes a quite different approach by exalting visionary leadership. For example, George Barna claims, "Realize that true ministry begins with vision."[5] I find that statement shocking in its boldfaced rejection of New Testament teaching. Surely love and serving are more valued than vision in the New Testament! If Barna were on the mission field, we would easily criticize him for syncretism, refilling Christian terms and values with pagan meanings and values. What does Barna mean by vision?

> Vision is a picture held in your mind's eye of the way things could or should be in the days ahead. Vision connotes a visual reality, a portrait of conditions that do not exist currently. This picture is internalized and personal. It is not somebody else's view of the future, but one that uniquely belongs to you. Eventually, you will have to paint that mental portrait for others if you wish the vision to materialize in your church.[6]

This is the common definition that one can find in the secular and now "Christian" leadership literature. In secular circles, we can find boldfaced assertions that control is the motivation for executives to pursue this kind of vision. For example, one author says the need driving the desire for vision is "the need to control the organization's destiny."[7] The problem for Christians who want to adopt this secular usage is that there is no such usage in the Bible for this kind of vision. The only place this kind of concept is mentioned is in negative contexts like the story of the tower of Babel (Gen 11). Their vision to build a tower was offensive to God and brought God's discipline. Many leaders' visions today are just like that: about a building or a program or a measurable aim. Many of them, I fear, are derived from the same sorry source that the vision for the tower of Babel was: from the well of human willfulness. As Jeremiah the prophet says, "They speak visions of their own minds, not from the mouth of the LORD" (Jer 23:16). The letter of James in the New Testament provides a needed corrective to this controlling view of the future:

> Come now, you who say, "Today or tomorrow we will go to such and such a town and spend a year there, doing business and making money." Yet you do not even know what tomorrow will bring. What is your life? For you are a mist that appears for a little while and then vanishes. Instead you ought to say, "If the Lord wishes, we will live and do this or that." As it is, you boast in your arrogance; all such boasting is evil. Anyone, then, who knows the right thing to do and fails to do it, commits sin. (Jas 4:13-17)

Of course, there is the oft-quoted proverb, "Where there is no vision, the people perish" (Prov 29:18 KJV). Those who use this to urge visionary leadership seem unaware of the biblical use of this word for "vision." "Vision" here is not "a visual picture that communicates the organizational goals and objectives" or "forward-looking, future-think, out in front of the people." These may be good things for Intel and Ford Motor Company, but they are not a part of the biblical record of how God leads his people. The NRSV translates this same verse in a way that better reflects this biblical understanding: "Where there is no prophecy [NIV "revelation"], the people cast off restraint, but happy are those who keep the law" (Prov 29:18). Biblical vision is not about a leader's architectural picture for what the people will accomplish together. Biblical vision is clearly and only *prophetic vision*, revelations that come from God supernaturally (for example, Gen 15:1; 46:2; Num 12:6; 1 Sam 3:1). This is the "dreams and visions" sort of vision, inspired and imparted by God to the person of his choosing (for example, Dan 2:28).[8] This is the spiritual gift that is promised to be restored in the church in the last days with the coming of Jesus. We can see this clearly when Peter interprets the spiritual activity of Pentecost in Jerusalem just after Jesus' resurrection. He cites the prophet Joel (Joel 2:28):

> *In the last days it will be, God declares, that I will pour out my Spirit upon all flesh, and your sons and your daughters shall prophesy, and your young men shall see visions, and your old men shall dream dreams.* (Acts 2:17)

It is clear that here, as elsewhere in the Bible, what is meant is Spirit-inspired, prophetic dreams and visions, as Peter goes on to cite Joel: "Even upon my slaves, both men and women, in those days I will pour out my Spirit; and they shall prophesy" (Acts 2:18). This is how the translated term *vision* is used more than one hundred times in the NRSV.

Dietrich Bonhoeffer, martyred seven days before the Allies liberated his prison camp at the end of World War II, rightly criticizes the secular conception of visionary leadership that has crept into the church.

> God hates visionary dreaming; it makes the dreamer proud and pretentious. The man who fashions a visionary ideal of community demands that it be realized by God, by others, and by himself. He enters the community of Christians with his demands, sets up his own law, and judges the brethren and God Himself accordingly. He stands adamant, a living reproach to all others in the circle of brethren.[9]

How much more blunt can you get? How many of us have experienced the drivenness of a leader having been caught up in his or her vision? I speak with some remorse and regret for times that my "visionary dreaming" has left me "proud and pretentious," judgmental and disapproving of the believers God had called me to shepherd and to care for. I have spoken with too many pastors who seem content to drive people out of their church because they do not fit with their vision. This is not the heart of the good Shepherd. How could Jesus be pleased when

a goal or a program is valued more than his precious sheep, the bride
for whom he died?

Instead, we should pray for a burden, God's heart for the world around
us. When you have God's burden, you always know what you need to do
next. When God reveals his mind and heart to his people, his word and
his will become reality. All of us are called to exchange our concerns and
the things that weigh us down for Jesus' heart and burden for the world:

> Come to me, all you that are weary and are carrying heavy burdens,
> and I will give you rest. Take my yoke upon you, and learn from me; for
> I am gentle and humble in heart, and you will find rest for your souls.
> For my yoke is easy, and my burden is light. (Mt 11:28-30)

Like many of the important truths of our life in God, so this truth is
paradoxical. We lay down our burdens, our agendas, and take on God's
"easy" and "light" yoke. Even though his is a burden for the world, it is
easy compared with ours because we are joining Jesus in his work. On
the other side of the yoke pulling with us is the powerful and almighty
resurrected One, carrying the weight of the world. It feels easier and
lighter because of who is helping carry the load. When we have God's
burden, we see people with eyes of compassion and difficult people as
our family and friends who have fallen into a ditch and need help getting out. When we have a burden, we gain God's heart for the people
we meet and the people we know. We no longer see them through the
eyes of what is wrong with them. We see them with God's eyes of mercy
and concern. When we have a burden, people are never a bother.

Joining What God Is Doing

Jesus practiced this sort of guidance. He was well aware of the religious
rules that sabbath is a day to shut down and do no physical effort of any
kind. Even so, this was the day God chose to heal a man who had been

ill for thirty-eight years. As a testimony to God, and as an act of trust and obedience, Jesus commanded him to carry his mat (Jn 5:1-47). As a result, the religious rule keepers "started persecuting Jesus because he was doing such things on the sabbath" (Jn 5:16).

What is Jesus' defense? "Jesus said to them, 'Very truly, I tell you, the Son can do nothing on his own, but only what he sees the Father doing; for whatever the Father does, the Son does likewise'" (Jn 5:19). He sets a clear example for us. How do we know what to do? We need to look for what God is up to, and join that.

This is the crucial doctrine of prevenient grace. It says that God is already at work. We do not need to seek to do something for God, because God is already there. We need to seek to join God, to work with God in what he is already doing. Paul describes his cooperation with Apollos in the ministry at Corinth in these terms: "For we are God's co-workers, and you are God's field, God's building" (i.e., not Paul's or Apollos's field or building; 1 Cor 3:9). Likewise, he sent Timothy to the Thessalonian church, "our brother and God's co-worker in the gospel of Christ" (1 Thess 3:2).

This is quite a different conception of frontline ministry than many pioneers have. We need to guard against the rugged individualism of the attitude, "I need to go and take God there." Instead, we need to discern and uncover what God is already doing so we can join his work. John Wesley, a great missionary practitioner of the eighteenth century, operationalized this approach at the early Methodist conferences when requests came for them to send preachers and missionaries. Wesley asked at those early meetings, "What evidence do we have that God is already at work in this place? Whom has God already raised up for this work? How can we join what God is doing?" These are the questions of effective missionaries. We are not rugged individualists planting the Christian flag on virgin soil asking, "Where can I go to make my mark?" We are God's coworkers, joining in with what God is doing, catching and flowing in the wind of God's Spirit, serving God's purpose in our generation.

Rick Warren calls this "catching the wave":

> Our job as church leaders, like experienced surfers, is to recognize a wave of God's Spirit and ride it. It is not our responsibility to *make* waves but to recognize how God is working in the world and join him in the endeavor. . . . The amazing thing is this: *The more skilled we become in riding waves of growth, the more God sends.*[10]

My sense is there are a lot of frustrated pastors out there who mistakenly have tried to "make waves" instead of learning this key, first principle of identifying and catching God's wave, what God is up to. Methods don't work and won't work when we have not learned how to be directed by the Spirit. Once we have learned to surf, methods become an effective tool for following through on what God has directed us to do. (Some suggestions are offered at the end of this chapter.)

What burden has God given you? For whom do you have a soul ache? Once you have it, you will have no problem identifying what God is up to so you can "catch the wave." A burden gives you an internal compass, so you always know what to do next to please your Lord.

A Personal Odyssey

When I was coming to my end of the phase of ministry in the flesh, I had one last dance with coming up with a vision instead of seeking God's guidance. I was pastoring two churches in the same village in England while I was completing my graduate work. Those two churches were made up of people who lived next to each other and roughly had the same problems facing them. Both congregations were too small for their facilities, so it seemed obvious that these two churches of the same denomination— merely a half mile apart—should pool their resources and worship and serve together on the "united we stand, divided we fall" principle.

In that part of the world, many churches have successfully joined together, but to this day I have no idea if that is what God wanted for those two churches. I am embarrassed to admit this, but it is true. I know I thought it made sense, I thought it reflected the values of the kingdom, and I thought it had potential to bring renewal from the one more lively congregation to the less lively one. Many in the two churches were in favor of it. Financially it made sense, since by the sale of property of two inefficient buildings with no parking at either we could make a good start on an attractive facility, and so forth.

We spent two years in conversations and explorations, with little prayer. This was not their fault. All the blame is on my shoulders. I was not following the Lord Jesus. I was not led by the Spirit. I was leading out of good ideas and consensus and process. I was doing a good job of leading and team building in a secular sense, but I failed in my responsibility to follow. When crunch time came, hidden agendas and the unwillingness of some influential people to leave "their building" submarined the process. The wheels came off, and it was only then that I realized that we had not consulted the Lord. An embarrassing story to tell, but I learned a painful lesson. I was like Joshua, who reasoned in his own wisdom with the Gibeonites but was chastised because he "did not inquire of the LORD" (Josh 9:14). I learned full well what Isaiah was talking about:

> *Oh, rebellious children, says the LORD, who carry out a plan, but not mine; who make an alliance, but against my will, adding sin to sin; who set out to go down to Egypt without asking for my counsel, to take refuge in the protection of Pharaoh, and to seek shelter in the shadow of Egypt. Therefore the protection of Pharaoh shall become your shame, and the shelter in the shadow of Egypt your humiliation. (Is 30:1-3)*

As the great Dutch Christian Corrie ten Boom has said, "When Christians have meetings, the devil smiles. When Christians make great plans, the devil laughs. When Christians pray, the devil trembles."

The next step in my growth came when we returned to the United States from England. I became pastor of a church that had much potential but had been through some difficult times. Before taking over pastoral responsibility, I met with church leaders to get acquainted and iron some things out. Still jet lagged from the trip, I awoke early one morning and jogged to the highest point I could see. On top of that hill I could see miles in every direction, west to a beautiful delta region and east to the miles of planned subdivisions waiting to be constructed. With my eyes I could see the opportunity and promise of the place. The church was perfectly situated to reach out to the thousands of new people moving there, and I have a deep passion for outreach and evangelism.

Something checked my spirit. It was God. I realized I was doing it again, imagining the possibilities and planning a vision in my flesh. By God's grace I stopped myself and prayed. Finally, I relented and asked, "Lord, give me your burden for this church and community." As the sun came up and the beauty of that valley surrounded me, my heart sank because the heavens were silent.

I was frustrated, disappointed and even doubting if I had made the right decision to come there. I trudged down the hill and dragged myself back toward home. I was truly silent and had stopped striving in my flesh for the first time. I felt broken and humbled. It was in that moment that a voice I had rarely heard said three simple words. It was the still, small voice of God: "Rebuild my house."

What did that mean? Why me? My call was to reach out to the lost. What was this assignment? How could I do it? Even though I was filled with questions and doubts, I began talking about this simple call that had come after I fell off my orchestrated mountaintop. Nevertheless, throughout that day and for the next two years, I pursued this burden that God had for his church in that area and not simply for the congregation for whom I was becoming pastor.

This congregation had been through two major splits in the previous few years. The last split was led by a friend of mine who had been on staff there. He had led many of the best givers and strongest leaders to start a new congregation in the same town. Acrimonious talk and broken relationships were the norm. Never had I seen such a broken church. The facilities reflected the two major divorces this church family had been through.

Even so, these were special people, God's children. They had a heart for Jesus, a passion for prayer and a deep desire to serve and reach out. I found myself relying on God like never before as I became mostly a pastoral counselor and interventionist leader. Everything seemed to be broken. Truly God's house—spiritually, relationally and physically—needed to be rebuilt.

It wasn't long before I started receiving the most painful kind of phone calls a pastor can get. Someone would call and say, "Hi, I used to go to your church. I am never going to go there again, but I need to talk about what happened with somebody." When I heard this, I had to say yes, even though my flesh would have said no. The echo of that still small voice extended to every living stone of the Lord's temple: "Rebuild my house." This call from God included ministering to those who lived in other rooms of God's house.

I estimate that I spent one hundred hours in such conversations with people the first six months I was there. They would spew out all sorts of hurt and unbelievable happenings, and I would listen, cry and pray with them. At the end they would say, "Thank you very much," and then proceed to tell me about their wonderful new church. We would say goodbye, and they would be on their way.

This is not the way to build a bigger congregation (at least, I have never heard or read anyone who said so). Yet our congregation grew significantly as God blessed simple steps of faith and obedience. Most important, I knew God was pleased with the spiritual and relational rebuilding of the body of Christ.

This extended to healing the breeches of relationships between our congregation and the new congregation that had formed. Because of the graciousness of their pastor, many links were established, many misunderstandings were healed, and I was even invited to speak at their Good Friday service.

Part of the rebuilding work God had in that place was getting together with pastors from other churches and to support the building of the one body of Christ in that town. This was something God was doing, and my arrival and assignment were a part of God's overall initiative. It was no surprise to learn that this was something stirring in the hearts of many pastors there too. When we join what God is doing, we find that there are others God is stirring in the same ways.

I was at that church only two years. From the start it seemed like I would be an interim pastor (another thing I would never have chosen for myself!). When I arrived, the patient was in intensive care, but by the time I left the congregation was being wheeled out of the hospital. During that time, I had been a remodeler, reshaping significantly the life and ministry of that congregation. I listened more, prayed more and was involved in more conflict that I ever would have chosen. It seemed like all the fun stuff didn't begin until after I left. But I have a good conscience that I had followed the Lord's directive and obeyed the burden he had given me. I can see how many God things have come out of that time, and I thank God that for once I had mostly sought the will of God instead of the will of Dodd.

Getting Over Good Ideas

The problem is that so many of today's Christian leaders lead out of good ideas. They have been to seminary and seminars; they have listened to the latest tapes and read the latest books. Wave after wave of fad after fad afflicts their thinking. Catching the wave of fads is quite different from catching the wave of God's Spirit. Many of these ideas and trends are helpful, but too often these ideas and ideals can be idols. What God is up to in a new, large, affluent, suburban church may have nothing to do with what God is doing in a transitional neighborhood where poverty is prevalent, or what the Spirit is stirring in a small town church with a long and rich heritage and set traditions. Completely different are campus and student ministries, which have changed significantly from what they were just a few years ago. Somehow we need to free ourselves from leading out of our heads, out of our good ideas. We need more than optimism or expectancy. We need a sense of what God is up to so we can yoke ourselves to his direction. There the work flows. When God is doing something and we join it, we find an ease and a delight in doing his work.

We need to replace our good ideas with God's ideas:

For my thoughts are not your thoughts, nor are your ways my ways, says the LORD. *For as the heavens are higher than the earth, so are my ways higher than your ways and my thoughts than your thoughts.* (Is 55:8-9)

As we make the shift to a posture of following, we give up on good ideas and hunger for God's ideas. When we have fully understood the bankruptcy of life in the flesh, when we have died to confidence in ourselves apart from God, when we have become disgusted with what our self-willed initiatives produce, we find ourselves hungry for God's guidance and direction. As we become more and more broken of our self-will, we become more and more able to receive God's direction and impulses. The still, small voice of God drowns out the loud racket of self-will and ego-building impulses.

Discerning God's Burden for Your Ministry

How do we discern God's wave and catch it? What burden has God laid upon you? We discern the answer to these questions in the life of prayer and among the body of Christ. The means of discernment are nothing new. In the process of seeking out God's direction, we must seek out God by use of the spiritual disciplines that cause our souls to mature and grow. Among these are

1. *Praying for a burden.* For whom do you have a soul ache? The statistics are shockingly low in how little pastors pray on a regular basis. How can we discern God's direction when we do not consult God? Pray for a burden. When God gives it to you, you will always know what to do next.

2. *Fasting for direction.* Throughout the life of Jesus we see the association of prayer, fasting and decision making. Fasting is a way to make space for God in your daily routine by slowing the pace and diminishing one's ego so that we are more responsive and can discern more clearly what God is up to. If you have never fasted as a part of your spiritual discipline, there are several good primers on the subject. Fasting was a practice of Jesus and the early church, often related to receiving ministry direction from God:

Now in the church at Antioch there were prophets and teachers: Barnabas, Simeon who was called Niger, Lucius of Cyrene, Manaen a member of the court of Herod the ruler, and Saul. While they were worshiping the Lord and fasting, the Holy Spirit said, "Set apart for me Barnabas and Saul for the work to which I have called them." Then

*after fasting and praying they laid their hands on them and sent them
off. (Acts 13:1-3)*

3, *Consulting the body.* We must rely on the wisdom of the body of
   Christ to find perspective and to rely on all the gifts that God has put
   in the community of Christians. Discerning what God is up to is not
   an individual thing that the leader does. It is a community thing that
   we all share.

4. *Searching the Scriptures.* This is a regular discipline that cultivates in
   us a heart receptive to God's kingdom mandates. A heart not steeped
   in the Scriptures is an arrogant heart that listens with the ears of ego
   and fancies of the flesh. Scripture's general directives and specific ap-
   plications can help us in discerning the mind of the Lord. God's plan
   for us will necessarily fit with God's desire to save the planet. As Andy
   Stanley says, "There will always be alignment between divinely orig-
   inated vision and God's master plan for this age. There will always be
   a correlation between what God has put in an individual heart to do
   and what he is up to in the world at large."[11] It might be possible in a
   secular way to have a vision that is self-centered and inward focused.
   When we get God's burden, it will be aligned with his passionate focus on the least, the last and the lost.

A Practical Tool As We Pray for a Burden

I direct a ministry called Share Jesus! in which we work with churches
and team members to help them formulate effective outreach strategies
by praying for a compelling burden. At the end of a prayer and planning
process, we bring a team of ten or so to work with them to implement
their new outreach strategy. I share the planning tool we use below because we have learned this approach can be adapted for any church
mission planning, not simply one of our Share Jesus! missions (feel free

to copy or adapt this for your setting). As you will see, we have not pitted prayer against planning, but we have prioritized following over planning, praying for a burden before planning a program. Planning and programming follow, but God's burden must be discerned first. Following is a portion of the cover letter we send to pastors who have invited a mission team to come to their church. Next is the instruction sheet, and it is followed by the worksheet.

1. Cover letter for pastors

Dear Pastor,

The most important part of your planning is the process, not the product. Gathering a team, prayer and discernment are the crucial elements. Together you will find God's guidance for your mission.

The Mission Planning Tool process is meant to push programming until last. First we want you to discern spiritually where you perceive God to be at work in your community and through your church. God is already doing something—what is it? How can you join what God is already doing? Toward this end, prayer and a "prayer survey" are crucial to your planning process (see the Instructions Sheet). Out of these will flow your Mission Burden and Objectives (numbers 2, 3 and 4 in the Worksheet).

You will need to consciously resist some temptations: the temptation to look inward to church programs and concerns instead of outward to community needs, the temptation to plan without praying it through and the temptation to pray without planning. Prayerful discernment as a group will never lead you wrong!

Your co-workers in Christ,
The Share Jesus! Team

2. *Instruction sheet*

INSTRUCTIONS FOR COMPLETING YOUR
MISSION PLANNING TOOL

We are glad you have decided to invite a Share Jesus! team to partner with your church.[12] Before we can assign leadership or a team,
we need to have a clear picture of your burden and objectives to
reach new people in your community. This tool provides the necessary next step for planning your mission. Here are the steps for
effectively completing this part of the planning.

Step 1: Gather the planning team.
It is very important that your mission is planned, developed and
implemented by a team of people. It cannot be left for the pastor
to do alone. An involved and committed planning team is a crucial part of the effectiveness of your mission. This group may be
an official group (the "evangelism committee" or the "council on
ministry"), but it is usually better to form a special team for the
purpose of your mission. Who has a heart for outreach? Who are
the opinion makers in your church whose support you need to
pull this off? Do you have a good mix of age, maturity and ministry
areas within the church? Who are new, emerging leaders who
could be involved in this new work? Are your young people repre-
sented?

Step 2: Commit yourselves to prayerful decision making.
The most effective missions we have seen are conceived and delivered in prayer. Begin by praying together as a group for guidance and direction in your planning of the mission, and commit

yourself to openness to God's leading in the process. Most importantly, ask God to give you a shared burden for unreached people in your mission target area: "Lord, break our hearts for the people who are breaking Your heart!"

Step 3: Do a prayer survey of your mission target area.
In groups of two or more, prayerfully walk or drive your mission field. Keep your eyes and hearts open to discern *who are the people near our church God is giving us a burden for?* Are there particular neighborhoods, locations (an apartment complex or a park) or people groups (nationality or age group) whom we are sensing a call to reach? Make sure you plan a debrief time when your prayerful scouting is reported back to your whole planning team. What are you sensing as a group?

Step 4: Agree on your mission's objectives.
See the detailed Worksheet.

3. Worksheet

SHARE JESUS!
MISSION PLANNING TOOL

1. *Our Mission Target Area.* Give a description of your immediate mission field after discussing it among yourselves (the conversation about this is a crucial part of the process). Are there many retired folks? Children or teenagers? What language groups and ethnic groups live here? Are there new housing developments, schools, parks or apartment complexes near your church? Is the population in your area growing, declining or

changing composition? Are there prominent employers in the area, or do many people commute to work? What else should be known about your area?

3. *Our Mission Burden.* For whom in our community do we feel a compelling burden? (see Instructions).

4. *Our Mission Purpose:* What new outreach and ministry do we plan to continue offering one year after our mission? How will we continue to reach out to those in #2 above?

5. *Our Mission Objectives:* What two to three specific objectives do we want to attain during the week of the mission to launch this ministry or these ministries we want to see in place one year later? (What objectives do you want to accomplish in the one week that our team is there to help you launch this new work?)

6. *What Preparations Do We Need To Make?* What preparations do we need to make to fulfill these mission objectives? How can we involve various people and segments of our congregation in all aspects of prayer, planning and development of this mission? What leaders need to be recruited or developed to accomplish this? What training or organization do we need to do in advance of the mission? How can we best publicize our mission activities to our community and to our church? What costs do we need to budget?

7. *What Are Our Follow-up Plans?* What will we need to do, plan and organize to effectively enfold the people reached during the mission into the life of our church? What new groups or classes must we launch as a result of an effective mission? What new class and group leaders do we need to recruit and equip to guide these new groups or programs?

Questions for Reflection and Discussion

What compelling burden is it that God has laid upon you? Your church? What is it inside you that you have to do as a Christian and as a group of Christians?

1. When you do a prayer survey of your area, for whom do you feel a deep concern or heart-breaking compassion? What do other leaders in your church sense?

2. Would you describe your church leadership more as driven or burdened? Why?

3. What do you notice God doing in your neighborhood and community? How can you join what God is doing?

4. What vision or visions do you have that may have become idols and need to be yielded on the altar of prayer so that you can hear afresh what God's heart is for you, your church and your community?

Notes

Chapter 1: Spirit-Empowered Leadership

[1] *The Orlando Sentinel*, Saturday, July 10, 1999.

[2] Among biblical scholars and theologians I have spoken with, there is a deep frustration with pop Christian leadership literature trading in concepts alien to biblical Christianity. Some recent and welcome exceptions are David Fisher, *The Twenty-first Century Pastor: A Vision Based on the Ministry of Paul* (Grand Rapids, Mich.: Zondervan, 1996); David Cannistraci, *Apostles and the Emerging Apostolic Movement: A Biblical Look at Apostleship and How God Is Using It to Bless His Church Today* (Ventura, Calif.: Renew, 1996); Helen Doohan, *Leadership in Paul* (Wilmington, Del.: Glazier, 1984); Robert Dale, *Leading Edge: Leadership Strategies from the New Testament* (Nashville: Abingdon, 1996). Dale, however, skips from Acts to the Pastoral Epistles, overlooking much of Paul's example of leadership.

[3] A revised version of my dissertation is now published as *Paul's Paradigmatic "I": Personal Example as Literary Strategy* (JSNTS 177; Sheffield: Sheffield Academic Press, 1999).

[4] Michael Riddell, *Threshold of the Future: Reforming the Church in the Post-Christian West* (London: SPCK, 1998), p. 3.

[5] Only China, India, Indonesia and Russia have more unchurched people than the United States. *Mission America*, January 1998.

[6] Brian Dodd, *The Problem with Paul* (Downers Grove, Ill.: InterVarsity Press, 1996).

[7] For an in-depth study of Paul's understanding of the Holy Spirit as the person, presence and power of God, see Gordon Fee's tour de force, *God's Empowering Presence: The Holy Spirit in the Letters of Paul* (Peabody, Mass.: Hendrickson, 1994).

Chapter 2: Followership and Self-Surrender

[1] The difficulty of deciding who is intended to be included in the "we" in 2 Corinthians is a notorious interpretive problem. Nevertheless, theologically speaking, Paul's "we" here includes you and me. Anyone who is competent to minister has been made so by God.

[2] This is the often-repeated assumption about Paul. A close reading of Acts undoes

this common misconception.

[3]Mike Yaconelli, *Dangerous Wonder: The Adventure of Childlike Faith* (Colorado Springs: NavPress, 1998), p. 28.

[4]"Stoichē," *Exegetical Dictionary of the New Testament*, ed. Horst Balz and Gerhard Schneider, 3 vols. (Grand Rapids, Mich.: Eerdmans, 1993), 3:278.

[5]James D. G. Dunn, *The Theology of Paul the Apostle* (Grand Rapids, Mich.: Eerdmans, 1998), p. 72.

[6]Martin Luther relates flesh and body in this way: "The term 'flesh' applies to a person who, in thought and in fact, lives and labours in the service of the body and the temporal life. The term 'spirit' applies to a person, who, in thought and fact, lives and labours in the service of the spirit and the life to come. Unless you give these terms this connotation, you will never comprehend Paul's epistle to the Romans, nor any other book of Holy Scripture" (*Martin Luther's Preface to the Epistle of St. Paul to the Romans* [Nashville: Discipleship Resources, 1977], p. 8).

[7]As John Wesley calls them in his sermon by that title.

[8]These "Judaizers" also could have been Gentiles who had been God-fearers and then had been circumcised prior to becoming Christians, and thus they may have stoutly defended the need for other Gentiles to submit to Jewish law as Jewish believers had.

[9]Charles H. Spurgeon, "David's Prayer in the Cave," in *Twelve Sermons on Prayer* (Grand Rapids, Mich.: Baker, 1990), p. 149.

[10]Ibid.

[11]For more information, contact Share Jesus! P.O. Box 196548, Winter Springs, FL 32719-6548. E-mail: Info@sharejesus.org.

[12]This is in addition to Paul's awareness of the use of *kyrios* in the Septuagint, the Greek translation of the Old Testament, as the most common translation for God's holy name, Yahweh.

[13]For an extended discussion of the images of slavery in Paul, see "The Slave of Christ and the Slaves of Antiquity" in Brian J. Dodd, *The Problem with Paul* (Downers Grove, Ill.: InterVarsity Press, 1996), pp. 81-110.

[14]For my extended interpretation of Galatians in light of Galatians 1:10, see "Christ's Slave, People Pleasers and Galatians 1:10," *NTS* 42 (1996): 90-104.

Chapter 3: Pay the Price, Carry the Cross

[1]Throughout this chapter I am discussing only the suffering that comes from pursuing faithful ministry. Of course we can suffer from our foolishness or disobedience. That is not what this chapter is about.

[2] Ernst Käsemann, "The Saving Significance of the Death of Jesus in Paul," in *Perspectives on Paul*, trans. Margaret Kohl (London: SCM Press, 1971), pp. 32-59 (37).

[3] *Sacramento Bee*, February 4, 1999.

[4] Eugene Peterson, Beeson Lecture at Asbury Theological Seminary, February 18, 1999.

[5] Peter Marshall, "A Metaphor of Social Shame: ΘΡΙΑΜΒΕΥΛΕΙΝ in 2 Cor 2:14," *NovT* 25 (1983): 302-17.

[6] Victor Paul Furnish, *2 Corinthians*, Anchor Bible 32A (New York: Doubleday, 1984), p. 173.

[7] Charles B. Cousar, *A Theology of the Cross: The Death of Jesus in the Pauline Letters* (Minneapolis: Fortress, 1990), p. 11.

[8] Church history might add to the list, in retrospect, martyrdom. According to tradition, Paul was beheaded in Rome.

[9] A story emailed to me by my friend Larry Marcon.

Chapter 4: God's Power in Cracked Pots

[1] Robert Greene and Joost Elffers, *The 48 Laws of Power* (New York: Penguin, 1998).

[2] Not her real name.

[3] Study by the National Center on Addiction and Substance Abuse at Columbia University, based primarily on 1999 data, AP News Service, ABCNews.com, January 26, 2000.

[4] Minnesota Governor Jesse Ventura, quoted in *U.S. Catholic*, December 1999, p. 10.

[5] I still wince when I recall a former pastor of mine who told me not to spend time helping a single mother with four children, since "she will never give anything back to the church." Is that why we love and care? So they will give something back to the church? I thought we love because he first loved us, even while we were dead in our sins!

Chapter 5: The Power of Personal Example

[1] Willis Peter de Boer, *The Imitation of Paul: An Exegetical Study* (Kampen, Netherlands: J. H. Kok, 1962).

[2] Brian J. Dodd, *Paul's Paradigmatic "I": Personal Example as Literary Strategy* (JSNTSS 177; Sheffield: Sheffield Academic Press, 1999).

[3] Wayne C. Booth, *The Rhetoric of Fiction* (Chicago: University of Chicago Press, 1983), p. 20.

[4]1 Cor 1:1, 12; 3:23; 4:1; 7:22; 15:23; cf. 2 Cor 10:7; Gal 3:29; 5:24.

[5]J. Robert Clinton, *The Making of a Leader: Recognizing the Lessons and Stages of Leadership Development* (Colorado Springs: NavPress, 1988).

Chapter 6: The Power of Partners

[1]On that score, a caricature of what is worst about "Christian" leadership literature is the book by Laurie Beth Jones, *Jesus CEO: Using Ancient Wisdom for Visionary Leadership* (New York: Hyperion, 1995).

[2]Jon R. Katzenbach and Douglas K. Smith, *The Wisdom of Teams* (New York: Harvard Business School Press, 1993), p. 9.

[3]See Victor Paul Furnish, "Fellow Workers in God's Service," *JBL* 80 (1961): 364-70.

[4]For a full treatment see Robert Banks, *Paul's Idea of Community: The Early House Churches in Their Historical Setting* (Grand Rapids, Mich.: Eerdmans, 1988).

[5]J. Paul Sampley, *Pauline Partnership in Christ: Christian Community and Commitment in Light of Roman Law* (Philadelphia: Fortress, 1980).

[6]T. R. Glover, *Paul of Tarsus* (London: SCM Press, 1925), pp. 178-83.

[7]E. Earle Ellis, "Paul and His Co-workers," *NTS* 17 (1971): 437-52. The best full-length treatment is in German: Wolf-Henning Ollrog, *Paulus und seine Mitarbeiter: Untersuchungen zu Theorie und Praxis der paulinischen Mission* (Neukirchen-Vluyn: Neukirchener Verlag, 1979).

[8]F. F. Bruce, *The Pauline Circle* (Grand Rapids, Mich.: Eerdmans, 1985), pp. 8-9.

[9]Ibid., p. 45.

[10]C. E. B. Cranfield, *The Epistle to the Romans*, 2 vols. (Edinburgh: T & T Clark, 1979), 2:788.

Chapter 7: Through Prayer

[1] Oscar Cullmann, *Prayer in the New Testament* (Minneapolis: Fortress, 1994), p. 73.

[2] Patrick D. Miller, *They Cried to the Lord: The Form and Theology of Biblical Prayer* (Minneapolis: Fortress, 1994), p. 325.

[3] E. M. Bounds, *Prayer and Praying Men* (1921; Grand Rapids, Mich.: Baker, 1977), p. 160.

[4] Quoted in Bounds, *Prayer and Praying Men*, p. 97.

[5] Bounds, *Prayer and Praying Men*, p. 151.

[6] Cullmann, *Prayer in the New Testament*, p. 81.

[7] David Rambo, "Pray First," in a CMA Church mailing, p. 15.

[8] Rom 1:9; 1 Thess 1:2; 2 Thess 1:11; 2:13; Phil 1:3; Col 1:3; 2 Tim 1:3.

[9] For example, Walter Wink, *Naming the Powers: The Language of Power in the New*

Testament (Philadelphia: Fortress, 1984). Wink embarks on an explicit journey to "demythologize" the demonic language in the New Testament. Many contemporary pastors and leaders are functionally where Wink is but less open and honest about it.

¹⁰C. S. Lewis, *The Screwtape Letters* (New York: Time, 1941), p. xxxi.

¹¹Francis MacNutt, *Deliverance from Evil Spirits: A Practical Manual* (Grand Rapids, Mich.: Chosen Books, 1995), p. 23.

¹²For a practical study in Jesus' example and teaching of how we can improve our prayer lives, see Brian J. Dodd, *Praying Jesus' Way: A Guide for Beginners and Veterans* (Downers Grove, Ill.: InterVarsity Press, 1997), p. 8.

Chapter 8: The Race to the Bottom

¹Andy Butcher, ed., "Holyfield Says He Will Win Title Rematch—and Quit at the Top," Charisma News Service 1, no. 182, November 10, 1999.

²See, for example, Gal 1:10, where *doulos* should be translated "slave," not "servant" as most North American translations have it. See Brian J. Dodd, "Christ's Slave, People Pleasing and Galatians 1:10," NTS 42 (1996): 90-104.

³See "The Slave of Christ and the Slaves of Antiquity," in Brian J. Dodd, *The Problem with Paul* (Downers Grove. Ill.: InterVarsity Press, 1996), pp. 81-110.

⁴Henri J. M. Nouwen, *In the Name of Jesus: Reflections on Christian Leadership* (New York: Crossroad: 1990), p. 17.

⁵Bill Thrall, Bruce McNicol and Ken McElrath, *The Ascent of a Leader: How Ordinary Relationships Develop Extraordinary Character and Influence* (San Francisco: Jossey-Bass, 1999). Though there is some profound and significant content in this book, from the perspective of Jesus' and Paul's self-lowering leadership, the title is a poor choice (and, to be fair, often out of an author's control, as in the case of the book you are reading). The subtitle of their book is excellent.

Chapter 9: The Leadership We Need Is Apostolic

¹Floyd McClung, "What Is Apostolic Passion?" in *Perspectives on the World Christian Movement Reader*, ed. Ralph D. Winters and Steven C. Hawthorne, 3rd ed. (Pasadena, Calif.: William Carey Library, 1981).

²See William Chadwick, *Stealing Sheep: The Church's Hidden Problems with Transfer Growth* (Downers Grove, Ill.: InterVarsity Press, 2001).

³Garrison Keillor, *Wobegon Boy* (New York: Penguin, 1997), p. 137.

⁴Christian A. Schwarz, *Natural Church Development: A Guide to Eight Essential Qualities of Healthy Churches* (Carol Stream, Ill.: ChurchSmart Resources, 1996).

Appendix: Hearing God's Direction for Your Ministry

1 For a detailed treatment, see Seyoon Kim, *The Origin of Paul's Gospel* (Grand Rapids, Mich.: Eerdmans, 1982).

2 His mysterious "thorn in the flesh" (2 Cor 12:7) might be thought to be his eye problem. The two problems with this identification are (1) Would Paul have called this problem a "messenger of Satan" (2 Cor 12:7)? (2) There have been more than two hundred proposals of what the "thorn in the flesh" might be. This should make us suspicious of any claim to certainty about its identity.

3 The definitive treatment is in German by Heinz Schreckenberg, *ANANKĒ, Untersuchungen zur Geschichte des Wortgebrauchs* (Zetemata 36; Munich: C. H. Beckesche, 1964).

4 The language about slavery in the New Testament is almost completely hidden in recent translations that use the less offensive and less Greco-Roman "servant." For an extensive treatment of this issue, see "The Slave of Christ and the Slaves of Antiquity," in Brian J. Dodd, *The Problem with Paul* (Downers Grove, Ill.: InterVarsity Press, 1996), pp. 81-110.

5 George Barna, *The Power of Vision: How You Can Capture and Apply God's Vision for Your Ministry* (Ventura, Calif.: Regal, 1992), p. 16.

6 Ibid., p. 29.

7 Benjamin B. Tregoe et al., *Vision in Action* (New York: Simon & Schuster, 1989), p. 23.

8 Compare the biblical usage with Andy Stanley's definition in *Visioneering*: "Visions are born in the soul of a man or woman who is consumed with the tension between what is and what could be. Any one who is emotionally involved—frustrated, brokenhearted, maybe even angry—about the way things are in light of the way they believe things could be, is a candidate for vision. Visions form in the hearts of those who are dissatisfied with the status quo" (Sisters, Ore.: Multnomah, 1999), p. 17. By this depiction, Paul was no candidate for a vision of Jesus on the road to Damascus. He had no apparent dissatisfaction with Judaism until Jesus' sovereign confrontation on that road.

9 Dietrich Bonhoeffer, *Life Together*, trans. John W. Doberstein (San Francisco: Harper & Row, 1954), p. 27.

10 Rick Warren, *The Purpose Driven Church: Growth Without Compromising Your Message and Mission* (Grand Rapids, Mich.: Zondervan, 1995), pp. 14-15.

11 Stanley, *Visioneering*, p. 26.

12 If you would like information about inviting a Share Jesus! team, contact Share Jesus! P.O. Box 6548, Winter Springs, FL 32719-6548. E-mail: Info@sharejesus.org. Web page <www.sharejesus.org>.

Subject Index

abuse doesn't nullify use, 35
accomplishment, success, 20, 22, 24, 148
alignment, 34
apostle, apostleship, 17, 52, 68, 74, 140-41, 151
apostolic, 150-57
appearance, image, 18, 20
Bible, Bible study, 15, 50
boast, 20
body of Christ, 23, 89, 108, 109-10
breaking, 47, 48, 49, 90, 91
brokenness, 47, 48, 49, 90, 91
call, 12, 139
cessationist, cessasionism, 28
Christ, in/of/into, 30, 97, 98, 101, 106, 109
church, 23, 89, 108, 109-10
community, 106-15
control, 35, 82, 83, 140, 142, 163
cross, 11, 12, 14, 62-77, 83
crucified, 11, 12, 14, 62-77, 83
cruciform, 12, 14, 62-77, 83
dependence, 22, 33, 142
despised, 20, 86
direction, God's will, 10, 159-75
disappointment, 75-77
discerning God's will, 159-75
divine incognito, 84
DNA principle of leadership, 100-101
domination, 35, 82, 83, 140, 142, 163
example, 93-103
faking good, 86-87, 92
fear of man, 54-58
financial support, 18
flesh versus Spirit, 13, 26, 33, 38-41, 44, 45,
    49, 51, 54, 66, 89, 125
Follower's Prayer (Merton), 58
followership, 31, 32, 33, 36, 37, 58, 63, 173
foolishness, 20, 86, 139
Four Laws of Perfectionistic Churches, 86-
    87, 92
gnostics, gnosticism, 93-94, 97
God's will, 159-75
gospel, 16
grace, 21, 22, 25, 71, 107

Holy Spirit, 24, 26, 27, 28, 29, 31, 34, 36, 38,
    40, 71, 123
humility, 20, 22, 31, 45, 46, 143-48
image, appearance, 18, 20
imitation of Paul, 95-100
inauthenticity, 86-87, 92
individualism, 104-10
kingdom of God, 11, 12, 23, 31, 101
leadership
    contemporary studies, 16
    practices, 16
    relational, 104-20
    secular, 11, 13, 20, 21, 33
    strategies, 11, 13, 20, 21, 33
left-brain rationalism, 35, 137
Lord, lordship, 51, 53, 54, 140-41, 161-62
manager, management, 33, 150
master Jesus, 51, 53, 54, 140-41, 161-62
mercy, 21, 22
Merton, Thomas, 58, 61
ministry "in the flesh," 13, 26, 33, 38-41, 44,
    45, 49, 51, 54, 66, 89, 125
mission, 149-57
model, modeling, 93-103
modeling Christ, 14
pain, 62-77
partner, partnership, 104-20
people pleasing, 54-58
persecution, 62-77
personal example, 93-103
power, 35, 82, 83, 140, 142, 163
power of the Spirit, 23-29, 32
prayer, 14, 121-38
pretense, 86-87, 92
prevenient grace, 49-50, 166-68
pride, 20, 24, 45, 46
professionalism, 124
prophecy, prophetic revelation, 164-65, 174-
    75
public speaking, 17
reference point, 10, 63
Reformation principle, 35
relational leadership, 104-20
relationships, 104-20
renewal, 15
salvation, 12, 29
Scripture, 50
self-sufficiency, 82

slave, slavery, 17, 51, 52, 53, 54, 115, 140-41, 161
slavery of Christ, 17, 51, 52, 53, 54, 115, 140-41, 161
Spirit, 24, 26, 27, 28, 29, 31, 34, 36, 38, 40, 71, 123
Spirit versus flesh, 13, 26, 33, 38-41, 44, 45, 49, 51, 54, 66, 89, 125
Spirit-empowered, 16, 18, 23, 24, 25, 26, 27, 28, 29, 34, 46, 48, 49, 50, 54, 123
Spirit-led, 13, 14, 23, 27, 29, 34, 37, 38
spiritual gifts, 23, 89, 109
spiritual warfare, 135-37

submission, 41-47, 49, 51, 142, 155-57
success. See accomplishment, success
suffering, 15, 47, 61, 62-77
surrender, 41-47, 49, 51, 142, 155-57
synergism, 105
team, teamwork, 104-20
tentmaking, 18
trials, 15, 47, 61, 62-77
vision. See prophecy, prophetic revelation
vision, visionary, 33, 34, 159-75
walking in the Spirit. See spirit-empowered
weakness, 20, 70, 74, 79-92, 139
world, worldly, 11, 13, 16

Scripture Index

Genesis
11, *163*
15:1, *164*
46:2, *164*

Numbers
12:6, *164*

Deuteronomy
21:23, *146*

Joshua
9:14, *169*

1 Samuel
3:1, *164*

Psalms
127:1, *50*

Proverbs
14:12, *40*
16:18-19, *45*
29:18, *164*

Isaiah
30:1-3, *169*
31:1, *13*
49:6, *151*
55:8-9, *173*

Jeremiah
23:16, *164*

Daniel
2:28, *164*

Joel
2:28, *165*

Matthew
5:10-12, *67*

5:11-12, *73*
6:24, *64*
9:38, *134*
11:28-30, *166*
18, *94*
20, *106*, *148*
20:20-27, *75*, *78*, *82*
20:20-28, *141*
20:21, *141*
20:25-26, *142*
20:26-28, *142*
24, *78*

Mark
8, *125*
8:32, *74*
8:33, *125*
8:34-38, *64*
13:5-27, *78*

Luke
9:23, *64*
11:43, *147*
15, *153*
18:1, *137*
21, *78*

John
3, *26*
3:8, *24*
5, *90*
5:1-47, *167*
5:16, *167*
5:19, *167*
12:32-33, *66*
13, *148*
13:2-11, *53*
13:3, *145*
13:3-17, *145*
13:12-17, *53*
13:15, *145*
13:17, *145*

Acts
1:8, *27*
2:11, *27*
2:17, *165*
2:18, *165*

2:22, *28*
2:24, *28*
3, *124*
3:12, *27*, *124*
3:16, *124*
4:7, *27*
4:33, *27*
6:8, *27*
7:22, *28*
7:58—8:1, *160*
8:3, *160*
8:4, *160*
8:26-40, *50*
9:1-9, *161*
9:1-31, *43*
9:13-14, *19*
9:18, *116*
9:27, *116*
10:38, *28*
13:1-3, *175*
13:2, *34*
13:2-4, *126*
13:4-5, *34*
14:6-7, *116*
14:23, *126*
15, *19*
16:6, *36*
16:7, *36*
16:9-10, *36*
16:10, *116*
16:19-24, *116*
16:25, *127*
16:37-38, *116*
17:1-10, *34*
18:1-3, *117*
18:24, *117*
20:5, *116*
20:22-23, *37*
20:36, *127*
22:1-21, *43*
26:1-23, *43*
27:1, *116*

Romans
1:1, *52*, *162*
1:9, *127*, *184*
5:6, *21*
6:16, *52*, *54*

6:22, *52*
7, *96*
8, *44*
8:5, *40*
8:5-9, *39*
8:7, *40*
8:9, *40*
8:12-27, *125*
8:13, *125*
8:14, *125*
8:16, *125*
8:18, *76*
8:26, *126*
8:26-27, *138*
8:35-37, *76*
12:2, *125*
12:12, *134*
15:18-19, *22*
15:26-27, *113*
15:30-32, *131*
16, *17*
16:1, *118*
16:3, *114*, *117*
16:6, *119*
16:7, *114*, *118*
16:9, *114*, *118*
16:12, *119*
16:21, *114*
16:22, *118*
16:23, *118*

1 Corinthians
1—2, *78*
1:1, *184*
1:9, *111*
1:11-13, *107*
1:12, *98*, *184*
1:18, *11*
1:18-31, *84*
1:22-24, *12*
1:27-29, *86*
1:27-31, *20*
2:1, *18*
2:3-5, *23*
3:4-9, *108*
3:7, *108*
3:9, *167*
3:21-23, *109*

3:23, 184
4, 69, 98
4:1, 184
4:9-13, 69
4:14-17, 96
4:15-17, 97
4:17, 98, 114
5, 107
5—10, 98
5:3, 97
6, 107
6:12, 98
7:7, 98
7:22, 52, 184
7:22-23, 141
8—10, 107
8:13—9:27, 98
9, 96, 147
9:16, 161
9:19, 52
10:16-21, 111
11, 89, 98
11—14, 107
11:1, 96, 98
11:1-2, 98
12, 109
12:4-6, 109
12:4-13, 23
12:8-11, 109
12:12-14, 109
12:15-18, 89
12:15-31, 109
12:18, 110
12:21-27, 89
12:21-31, 110
13, 110
14:15, 126
15, 108
15:23, 184
16:19, 117

2 Corinthians
1:15—2:13, 37
2:12, 37
2:14, 69, 183
3:5, 32
3:6, 32
4:5, 52, 162

4:6, 81
4:7, 32, 50, 81
4:7-11, 70
4:8-9, 75
4:10, 71
4:16-17, 75
4:17, 77
5:17, 30
6, 76
6:14, 112
8:3-5, 113
8:23, 114
9:13, 113
10, 25
10:1, 19
10:3-4, 137
10:3-5, 25
10:7, 184
10:10, 18, 73
11, 76
11:4, 74
11:5, 73
11:22, 73
11:24, 76
11:25, 76
11:28, 76
11:30, 74
12:7, 186
12:7-10, 75
12:9, 81
12:9-10, 25
12:11, 26
12:12, 26, 73
13:3, 73
13:13, 111

Galatians
1—2, 19, 96
1:10, 54, 55, 162, 182, 185
2, 19
2:1, 117
2:9, 113
2:11-15, 55
2:14, 55
2:19-20, 71
3:2-4, 26
3:13, 146

3:29, 184
4:3, 52
4:6, 125
4:12, 96
4:13-14, 18
4:15, 161
5:11, 71
5:16-18, 27
5:17, 38
5:24, 184
5:25, 37
6:6, 112
6:9, 75
6:11, 161
6:12, 71
6:17, 161

Ephesians
1:16, 127
1:16-19, 129
3:13, 71
3:16-19, 129
4:32, 96
5:21-33, 111
6:10-18, 136
6:18, 134
6:19-20, 133

Philippians
1:1, 52, 162
1:3, 184
1:3-5, 130
1:5, 112
1:18-19, 130
2, 106, 148
2:5-11, 145
2:7, 52
2:9, 146
2:19-30, 115
2:25, 112, 114, 118
2:30, 112
3, 43
3:3-5, 18
3:3-11, 43, 44
3:4, 44
3:4-8, 147
3:7, 18
3:8, 44

3:10, 45
3:10-11, 72
3:17, 96, 99
4:2-3, 114, 118
4:3, 114, 118
4:6, 135
4:9, 96, 99
4:14-18, 113

Colossians
1:3, 184
1:3-4, 130
1:7, 114, 118
1:9, 128
1:24, 72
2:15, 75
3:12, 49
4, 118
4:2, 134
4:2-4, 133
4:7, 114, 118
4:9, 118
4:10, 114, 118
4:11, 114, 118
4:12, 52, 128
4:14, 114, 116, 118

1 Thessalonians
1:1, 34
1:2, 184
1:2-3, 130
1:5-6, 25
1:6-7, 72, 96, 99
2:2, 116
2:4-6, 57
2:7, 19, 49
2:13-14, 99
2:14, 96
3:2, 167
3:2-5, 115
3:10, 128
5:16-18, 135
5:25, 131

2 Thessalonians
1:5, 72
1:11, 184
2:1, 34

2:13, 184
3:1, 133
3:6-9, 99
3:7-9, 96

1 Timothy
1:2, 116
1:7, 29
1:12-17, 21
1:13, 19
1:15, 19
1:15-16, 90
2:1, 135
2:8, 135
4:12, 96
4:12-16, 100

2 Timothy
1:3, 128, 184

1:8, 19, 64, 72
1:11-12, 72
1:12, 64
1:15, 64
1:16-18, 119
2:1-2, 119
2:3, 64
2:9, 64
2:24, 49, 52
3:5, 29
3:10-12, 72
3:11, 64
3:11-12, 65
3:12, 73
3:16-17, 16
4:5, 64
4:10, 118
4:11, 116
4:19, 117

Titus
1:1, 162
1:4, 117
2:7-8, 96, 100
3:6, 28

Philemon
1, 114, 118, 162
1—2, 115
1:24, 114
2, 114, 118
17, 113, 115
22, 131
23, 114, 118
24, 116, 118

Hebrews
4:16, 138
7:25, 138

13:12-13, 152

James
4:13-17, 164

1 Peter
4:12-14, 78

1 John
4:1-2, 94